Contents

Introduction

This book is a collection of the detailed histories of some emirates and towns in KinNupe. This is another first of its kind. There is hardly any other book that have collected the histories of major Nupe emirates and towns together in one volume like this.

More interesting is the fact that the history of each of the Nupe emirate or town featured in this book is narrated in such details that can hardly be gotten anywhere else.

Furthermore, this is the first time an attempt is made at a 'decolonized' version of the histories of these Nupe Emirates and towns. All along all the historical account of these towns have been sketchy and brief histories garnered mostly from the inaccurate and biased historical records and gazetteers of Colonial scribes and resident officers in the 20th centuries. This book is the first deliberate break away from that Colonial practice.

The major Nupe emirates featured in this book include those on both side of the River Niger, that is, in both Niger State and Kwara State. These include the Bida, Patigi, Agaie, Lafiagi, Lapai and Tsaragi Emirates. This is the first time the histories of each of these emirates is being told in exhaustive details.

Not all the histories of all the Nupe Emirates in KinNupe have been treated in this first edition of this book. The plan is that the histories of more Nupe Emirates and more towns throughout KinNupe will gradually be added in subsequent editions in the future.

Dr. Ndagi Abdullahi Amana Nupe
International Institute for Nupe Studies,
Bida, Nigeria.
5th April 2021

AGAIE

Mama

The first people to live in the place we call Agaie Emirate today are the prehistoric Nupe people known as the Mama. These Mama Nupe people were actually not only restricted or confined to the general area of today's Agaie Emirate but where spread over virtually the whole of ancient KinNupe and even beyond. They were a powerful and multitudinous race and that is why the word Mama, or Manman as we wrongly write it today, has survived into even Modern Nupe Language as referring to something large or great.

These Mama aboriginal Nupe people were the same that were mentioned as the Demdem or El-Demdem by the Arab historian El-Bakri as far back as 1067 AD. These Mama were also the ones whose lands who were known to the ancients as the Mina or, as the Arab geographers in Islamic Spain called them, Al-Mina. These Mama Nupe people were the same who erected a colossal statue of a goddess which came to be known as the Al-Mina Colossus or, as Sultan Bello wrongly pronounced it, Amina. And, hence, the origin of the story of Queen Amina of Zaria who was, in fact, a Nupe princess who was born, bred, flourished and died at Dunguru or today's Zungeru here in Central KinNupe.

The Mama Nupe people were also known as the Mara, Mala or, as the Latin Americans came to pronounce it, Male and, hence the generic name of the Nupe slaves and their descendants in the Americas to this very day.

In any case the Mama Nupe people were among the first people to inhabit and populate KinNupe in general and the area of today's Agaie in particular.

The Mama Nupe people were still a dominant population in the Agaie general area right unto barely historical times until the rise of the famous AtaGara Empire of the Zhitako Nupe people who came to displace the Mamas from Central KinNupe including the place where we have the Agaie Emirate today.

The Zhitako Nupe people had to fight endless wars with the Mama Nupe people before the latter were eventually subdued as their population was drastically reduced while many of them simply moved out of Central KinNupe and the Agaie area.

But as the Zhitako people took possession of the Agaie and as their population began to increase, they came into conflict with another equally ancient and indigenous Nupe people known as the Gara Nupe people. These Gara, as we shall discuss in the next heading, were in fact the founding half that merge with the Akanda, the other half, to form the United Kingdom of AtaGara.

Gara

In the beginning there were a very ancient Nupe people called the Gara. They derived their national name progressively from Gara, Gwara, Kwara or Koro which has always been the name of the River Niger since time immemorial. They derived their name from the River Niger because they have always been a people based on the banks of the River Niger right here in Central KinNupe since the beginning of time.

Sultan Bello pronounced Gara as Gawara. The Nupe national name Gara or Gwara was also pronounced as Agwara, Agwari or Gwari, Gbwari, Ibwari, Ibari or Ibara. Professor J.E.G. Sutton wrote that this Nupe Gara, Gwari or Ibara was the original and 'bedrock' race from which almost all the other tribes and ethnicities of ancient Nigeria were derived.

Professor J.E.G. Sutton also observed that the Gwari Nupe people should not be mistaken for the Gbari and Gbagyi people.

This Gara, Gwari or Ibara Nupe people established a kingdom bearing the same name, that is, Gara. And the king of the Gara Kingdom was known as the Garaki or, as we pronounce it today, Garki.

The Garki was also known as the Garani or, simply, as the Gani.

To this very day the festival of Gani has survived among the Nupe people of Kutigi. But Gani is also practiced among the Gbagyi, Borgu and the Borno people and, in fact, the Gani used to be a festival practiced and celebrated by so many ancient Nigerian peoples in very ancient times.

In any case this Gara, Gwari or Ibara Nupe people were the original or autochthonous people indigenous to the place where we have the Agaie Emirate located today. In other words, one of the most ancient people who inhabited today's Agaie Emirate in prehistoric times were the ancient Nupe people known variously as the Ibara, Gara or Gwari Nupe people.

As a matter of fact, so indigenous were these Gara Nupe people to the Agaie general area that even the name 'Agaie' is itself originally derived from the national name of the Gara Nupe people. The Gara people were also known as the Agaranye. The truth, actually, is that Agaranye simply means 'The Gara Person' as 'nye' was the Old Nupe affix in reference to a person.

But Agaranye was frequently shortened into Aganye which is the same that the Colonial Whitemen scribes came and wrongly transcribed as Agaye or Agaie.

Agaranye or Aganye was also pronounced as Agaya and in fact the Gara Nupe people, and the people of the general area of today's Agaie Enirate, were popularly referred to as the Agaya for a very long time. With their national name as the Agaya the kings of these people were officially known as the EtsuGaya or Etsugaya which is the same royal title that did survived among the people of the village of Rukwaji, some eight kilometers from Agaie town, as 'Tswagayaci' right unto modern historical times.

These Gara or Agaya Nupe people were so great a people in ancient times that they, once upon a time, populated virtually the whole ancient Northern and Middle Belt Nigeria combined. For one, Leo Africanus categorically documented the fact that the whole of Northern Nigeria was dominated by the Gara or Agaya Nupe people as recent as the end of the 16th century.

So great were the Gara or Agaya Nupe people in ancient times that the Kano traditions relate to this day that Kano was originally founded by these ancient Nupe people referred to in the Kano Chronicle as the Abagayawa.

In any case these Gara or Agaya or Agaya Nupe people were among the original inhabitants of the general area of the Agaie Emirate of today.

But with time another ancient Nupe people, called the Epa, migrated into today's Agaie Emirate general area. These Epa people partly displaced and partly intermixed with the autochthonous Ibara, Gara or Gwari Nupe people who were the original inhabitants of today's Agaie area.

Epa

The Epa came as invading conquerors and they with time subjugated the indigenous Gara Gwari Nupe people. The Epa were ardent warriors and they eventually founded and established their own kingdom called Epa Kingdom in the general area where we have the Agaie Emirate today. This Epa Kingdom grew into an almighty Epa Empire over the times.

The Epa Empire was the dominant superpower throughout the Central Sudan in very ancient times. Because it exercised sovereignty over a very large area corresponding to more or less the whole of ancient Nigeria, this Epa Empire of the Nupe people was known with so many different names to so many different ancient Nigerian peoples. The Idoma and Igala people called it Apa or Wapa or Wapan; the Yoruba people call it Ifa or Ife or Ile Ife; the Nupe people call it Epa;

the Edo-Benin people call it Uhe; the Igbira people call it Efa or Afa; and so on and on. And, interestingly enough, all these people said that they originated from this ancient Nupe Empire of Epa in very ancient times.

This Nupe Empire of Epa was mentioned, as 'Opu', by the Portuguese traveler Duarte Pacheco Pereira in 1505. Though the truth is that by the year 1505 the Epa or Opu Empire was already on the decline and had by then long past its glorious days.

The Epa Empire was dealt a death blow in the late 13th century when Tsudi (Tsoede) initiated his extensive Tsudi Wars from the 1250s onwards. In those days Tsudi brought his Akanda people down to today's Central KinNupe including the Agaie general area of today. The Akanda people who came with Tsudi from his paternal AtaGara Empire came to displace the Epa and the Mama Nupe peoples from most parts of Central KinNupe including the area of today's Agaie Emirate.

These Akanda people who came with Tsudi from AtaGara are the same people that are variously known to us today as the Ganagana and Dibo Zhitako people.

AtaGara

At a time, and as we mentioned earlier, the indigenous Gara people merged with the Ata or Akanda people to form the United Kingdom of AtaGara. The first dynasty of the AtaGara Empire was a Gani dynasty and the first emperors of the AtaGara Empire were actually known as the Gani.

It is in this regard that, as late as the latter half of the 15th century, when the first Portuguese sailors arrived the Benin Kingdom, the Oba of Benin was telling them that the Benin people are the subject of the 'Ogane'. The Benin pronounced the ancient Nupe royal title Gani or Agani as the Ogani which is what the Portuguese transcribed as Ogane.

The emperor of the AtaGara Nupe Empire was initially known as the Gani. The royal title Gani also became a national name of a greater section of the KinNupe that was directly under the territorial sovereignty of the Gani king of the Gara Kingdom. This Ganiland was also known as Ganyi or Ganye or Gaya or Agaya. It is this ancient name, Ganye, that the Colonial scribes came and transcribed as 'Gaie' or 'Agaie'.

Agaie was, in former times, a national name of by and large the whole of KinNupe. It was only in recent historical times that the name Agaie became reduced to that of a specific town.

The Ganagana and Dibo People of Agaie
The Gara people were also known as the Gana. Mary Meyerowitz wrote that the name of the ancient Ghana Empire

was derived from this ancient national name, Gana, of the Nupe people in very ancient times. As I discussed in my book, 'Gadunguru: How the Ghana Empire Originated from Nupe', the ancient Ghana Empire was actually founded by an ancient Nupe people.

In any case the Gara people were also known as the Garagara or Ganagana peoples. And the people of AtaGara Kingdom were also known as the Zhitakoro or Zhitako people. Of course AtaGara and AtaKoro or Takoro are one and the same name considering the fact that Koro and Gara are one and the same word pronounced differently by different tongues.

The people of the ancient Nupe kingdom of AtaGara or AtaKoro or Takoro were known as the Zhitakoro or Zhitako. The Shintakoi people, who are today classified as a Gbagyi people, were originally a Zhitako or ZhitaKoro or AtaGara Nupe people. But, and in any case, the Gbagyi and the Nupe people used to be one and the same people until very recent historical times, specifically around the time of the advent of the Fulani Jihadists who came and segregated the ancient Nupe Nation into Gbagyi and Nupe sub-nations.

These Zhitako, together with their precursory Gara, Gana or Ganagana peoples, were the major inhabitants of the territorial land of the AtaGara Kingdom known as Ganiland or Agani or, as we write it today, Agaie.

Don't forget that Agaie in those days refer to virtually the whole of KinNupe and, accordingly, the whole of ancient KinNupe was actually populated by the Ganagana and the Zhitako peoples. These same Ganagana or Zhitako people are the ones that are known as the Dibo Nupe people today. A number of scholars and researchers wrote that in former times the whole of KinNupe, including the place where we have the Bini city of Bida today, was originally populated by the Ganagana and Zhitako people combinely known as the Dibo people today.

The Dibo people initially occupied the whole of KinNupe and were in those days, and according to Professor A.H.M. Kirk-Greene, far larger in population than the minority Nupe subtribe we see them as today.

Agaie or Ganiland was also known as KinTako because of the location of the headquarters of the AtaGara or AtaKoro or Takoro or Tako Kingdom in it.

It was the rise of Tsoede's Nupeko, Nupekoro or Kororofa Empire in the 1250s that led to the fall also of the AtaGara Empire and the demographic decline and the displacement of the Dibo peoples out of all parts of ancient

KinNupe until they became confined to southeastern KinNupe as we see them today. And that was how the name Agaie or Ganiland became associated with only the southeastern part of KinNupe in historical times.

Before the rise of the Dibo peoples – in the form of the Ganagana and the Zhitako – and their subsequent spread over Central KinNupe and beyond, Central KinNupe was occupied amd inhabited by the ancient Yisa, Gwasa or Bassa Nupe peoples and the Epa, Apa, Ife or Nupe Nupe peoples of old. It was the Bassa Kingdom of the ancient Yisa Nupe people and the Apa Kingdom of the ancient Ife or Nupe Nupe people that the AtaGara Kingdom of the Ganagana and Zhitako Nupe people came and displace out of Central KinNupe.

That was how the Ganagana and Zhitako Dibo people came to occupy Central KinNupe and remained the dominant population and ruling people of Central KinNupe for a very long time spanning a century or so.

It is also in this same regard that we see that the place where we have the Agaie Emirate today was formerly dominated by a high population of the Ganagana and Dibo Zhitako Nupe people, otherwise known as the Akanda, who had earlier on came to partly displace and partly intermixed with the aboriginal Ibara, Gara or Gwari Nupe population that had earlier on dominated the population of this same place where we have the Agaie Emirate today.

Gbara

The Gara, Ganagana and Dibo Zhitako people were all of the general Ibara or Gara Nupe stock which was known to Nupe historians as the Gwagba Nupe people. The capital city of these Gwagba Nupe people was Gbara which was, by the end of the 18th century, ruled over by Etsu Jimada who was the head of the Gara or Ibara Nupe people in those days.

When Etsu Majiya II became the undisputed Etsu Nupe of the entire Nupe Nation in 1820s after defeating and killing his arch-rival Etsu Jimada at Ragada, the same Etsu Majiya embarked on the consolidation and expansion of his sovereignty over the whole of the Nupe Nation of those days. That was how Etsu Majiya II eventually subjugated both the Ganagana, Dibo or Zhitako people and their rival Epa people.

Before his subjugation of the Zhitako and Epa warring rivals, the Zhitako and Epa people of the general area of today's Agaie Emirate were originally under the nominal sovereignty of Etsu Jimada who was the Etsu Nupe ruling over the Eastern half of the Nupe Nation after the Nupe Nation shattered into two opponent kingdoms upon the death of Etsu Mamman in 1796.

Etsu Majiya II was still the almighty Etsu Nupe ruling over the people of the place we have the Agaie Emirate today when the Fulani Mallams began to gain ascendancy to political power in KinNupe at the end of the 18th century.

The Jihadists

The Ganagana were still inhabiting their southeastern KinNupe as Agaie and the Zhitako were still inhabiting the same southeastern KinNupe as KinTako when the Islamic Revolution burst out in KinNupe at the end of the 18th century.

By the end of the 18th century, somewhere around 1796, Shehu Abdurrahman Gbaji had declared his Islamic Jihad enterprise and he soon overwhelmed the whole of the Nupe Nation with his revolutionary Jihad warfare as he gadded about from one part of KinNupe to another with his mighty army of Jihad mercenaries.

The Nupe Jihadists were the first, in the whole of the Central Sudan, to come up with the idea of establishing a Central Sudan-wide Caliphate. The idea of a Nupe Caliphate that will replace the Songhai Empire and rule over the whole of the West African sub-region immediately transformed KinNupe into a magnet for all manners of Islamic scholars, Jihad mercenaries and Muslim divines from all parts of the Central Sudan and even beyond.

That was what brought Mallam Dendo or Manko of Raba, Man Musa Kodogi of Bida, Mallam Maliki of Lafiagi, Mallam Alimi of Ilorin, Mallam Babba of Agaie, and a countless other such itinerant Mallams to KinNupe at the end of the 18th century and at the beginning of the 19th century.

Mallam Babba, the founder of the Agaie Emirate, was originally from the village of Yantumaki in today's Katsina State. He came into KinNupe to seek his fortune as a Jihadist mercenary as was the fashion for most Islamic scholars in those days. He met Mallam Dendo, Man Musa Kodogi and other Mallams at Zugurma under Etsu Zubairu Majiya II.

The Mallams assisted Etsu Zubairu Majiya II in his dynastic struggle against Etsu Jimada who was eventually killed at the Battle of Ragada in 1826. Then Etsu Zubairu Majiya II assisted the Mallams in routing and eventually murdering their rival Shehu Abdurrahman Gbaji at the village of Kere in 1829.

But back in Raba the group of Mallams under Mallam Dendo became too powerful and a threat to the sovereignty of Etsu Zubairu Majiya II who eventually chased them out of Raba from whence they fled to Ilorin where they sought asylum under the protections of Mallam Alimi.

At Ilorin the Mallams invited Etsu Idirisa, the son of the Etsu Jimada who was killed by Etsu Zubairu Majiya II. The Mallams then rallied round Etsu Idirisa at Ilorin as they mobilised and prepared for an all-out war against Etsu Zubairu Majiya II.

Etsu Zubairu Majiya II attacked the Mallams and Etsu Idirisu at Ilorin and the result was the Battle of Ilorin also known as the Mugba Mugba Battle.

But Etsu Zubairu Majiya II lost the Battle and was actually chased by the Mallams across the River Niger back to Raba and thence to Zugurma.

After the Battle of Ilorin Mallam Dendo went back and settled at Raba while other Mallams went and settled in various other places. Mallam Maliki went and settled at Lafiagi and Mallam Babba went and settled at Agaie among the Ganaganas and the Zhitako people combinely known today as Dibo peoples.

Agaie Emirate
The story is that after the Battle of Ilorin, Mallam Babba followed Mallam Dendo back to Raba. He lived there in Raba with Mallam Dendo until one day Mallam Dendo advised him to go out and carve for himself an independent and sovereign Emirate.

Mallam Babba then left with twelve men in the direction of Diboland, that is the southeastern part of KinNupe inhabited by the Ganagana and the Zhitako Dibo Nupe peoples. Mallam Babba and his twelve stalwarts were actually hiding during the day and only journeyed during the night. They were afraid of being apprehended and arrested by the forces of the defeated Etsu Zubairu Majiya II who was still nursing his wounds and looking for any way to deal with any of the Fulani Mallams that he can lay his hands on.

At last, and after crossing three rivers, so the story goes, Mallam Babba eventually settled at a place called Eko Chekpa. This Eko Chekpa is just some five kilometres away from the present town of Agaie. In those days this area was completely a land of the Ganagana and Zhitako Dibo peoples and it was among these ancient Nupe peoples that Mallam Babba settled.

Mallam Babba settled down at Eko Chekpa among the Ganagana and Zhitako Dibo peoples and spent some time thinking of how to initiate his Jihad warfare through which he will conquer territories for his own emirate. His major problem was getting a capable war general who will lead the Jihad warfare for him since he, Mallam Babba, was already getting old.

But then a few years after settling down among the Dibos at Eko Chekpa, Mallam Babba heard of the death of another Fulani man, called Jauro who was actually the Diko or head of the Fulani peoples of Zaria, at Maza.

Jauro had come with his cattle and family to graze in the fertile land of KinNupe when he died at Maza. This Maza was a small village not that far away from Agaie. Furthermore, Jauro was also from the village of Yantumaki in Katsina, the same Yantumaki village from which Mallam Babba originally came. So, Mallam Babba went to Maza for the funeral of Jauro.

At Maza Mallam Babba met and became good friends with Umaru Yerima, the son of the late Jauro. This Umaru Yerima is the same that is known to history today as Daudu Maza and as the founder of the Lapai Emirate.

A couple of months after his father's funeral Daudu Maza visited Mallam Babba at Agaie. Mallam Babba then saw in the personality of Daudu Maza the war general he had long sought after. He asked Daudu Maza to be his war general and Daudu Maza did not object to the request. Soon the two reached an agreement to wage Jihad wars with Daudu Maza as the temporal head and Mallam Babba as the spiritual head of the Jihad campaign.

Mallam Babba then built his army from the original twelve men into a gargantuan army by mobilising warriors and mercenaries from Raba, Ilorin, and other areas.

The duo of Mallam Babba and General Daudu Maza began their Jihad warfare in earnest. General Daudu Maza was an able warrior and capable leader. In the beginning the Agaie army headed by General Daudu Maza had to fight battles on two fronts, first against the forces of Etsu Zubairu Majiya II under whose sovereignty the Eastern Half of KinNupe, including Diboland, falls and, secondly against the local forces of the indigenous Ganagana and Zhitako warriors who were defending their villages against the attack of the Agaie army.

But General Daudu Maza was able to successfully lead the Agaie army of Mallam Babba to defeat the forces of Etsu Majiya II and to conquer many villages throughout the length and breadth of Diboland and even beyond. He effectively conquered the Bataland, Katsaland and the Pai section of Gbagyiland.

As a matter of fact Agaie Emirate suddenly appeared on the map of KinNupe as the most vibrant and fastest growing emirate in the whole of the Nupe Nation. Within the spate of a few years the able General Daudu Maza had established an Agaie Emirate whose territorial expanse extended from the reaches of the River Kaduna to the northwest and down to the Baro-Gulu-Katcha area in the southeast. This, indeed, was a large emirate.

It was only in latter time, with the founding of the Lapai Emirate and the rise of the Bida Emirate, that most of the lands that initially belonged to the Agaie Emirate were taken over by other Nupe emirates including, most especially, the voraciously land-grabbing Bida Emirate.

Actually the sudden and rapid growth of the Agaie Emirate came to an end in 1827 when, after conquering the Dibo town of Fogbe for Mallam Babba, the Agaie War General Daudu Maza broke away from Mallam Babba and went and established his own Lapai Emirate some 18 miles to the northeast of Agaie.

The subtle point here, which is often missed by most people and overlooked by most research workers, is that the Agaie Emirate would have been the largest and most powerful Emirate in KinNupe but for the breakaway of Daudu Maza from Mallam Babba when the former left to go and form his own Lapai Emirate. In the beginning the territorial expanse of the Agaie Emirate was even larger than that of the Raba Emirate and even that of the Bida Emirate before the expansionist wars of Etsu Masaba the Great.

With the breakaway of General Daudu Maza, Mallam Babba could not get another able war general who could carried on with the innumerable conquest and rapid expansion of the Agaie Emirate. Instead Mallam Babba then focused on the consolidation of the power and sovereignty of the Agaie Emirate.

It was also around that time that Mallam Babba sent his brother, Mallam Suleman, to Gwandu to obtain the Flag of Recognition from the Gwandu authorities of Shehu Abdullahi Fodio thereby placing the Agaie Emirate under allegiance to the Gwandu half of the Sokoto Emirate.

In 1832 Mallam Babba turbaned his son, Abdullahi, as the first Emir of the Agaie Emirate. Mallam Babba as the regent actually remained as the de facto ruler of the Agaie Emirate for as long as he lived.

In 1841 Etsu Usman Zaki, fleeing from Raba, sojourned at Agaie. He was welcomed and accommodated by Mallam Babba who treated him as his own son due to Mallam Babba's cordial relationship with Usman Zaki's late father, Mallam Dendo.

Usman Zaki's junior brother, Masaba and Etsu Tsado of the Tsoede dynasty, have jointly attacked and devastated Raba in the disastrous Battle of Raba in 1841. Usman Zaki had to run for his dear life. He first sojourned at Agaie before he eventually left for Gwandu on exile.

Mallam Babba died in 1847.

Emir Abdullahi then effectively ruled Agaie Emirate and became renowned as a great and powerful ruler. He actually and further built Agaie into a great power in KinNupe rivaled only by the Dendo's dynasts' Emirate then at Raba. So powerful did Agaie became in those days that it was regarded and respected as a supreme military power throughout KinNupe and beyond.

In fact, and when the tide of war turned against Umaru Bahaushe, he besought Emir Abdullahi of Agaie to help him against Umaru Majigi and his other enemies during the siege of the small Bini walled village of Bida in 1856. But Emir Abdullahi of Agaie refused to help Umaru Bahaushe and that, in part, contributed to the defeat of Umaru Bahaushe.

Emir Abdullahi lived to be a very old man and he died in 1855.

Mamman Dikko was turbaned as the new Emir of Agaie in 1855. He was the son of the late Emir Abdullahi and was, accordingly, a grandson of Mallam Babba the founder of the Agaie Emirate.

Mamman Dikko was a royal personality right from birth and was groomed for rulership and royalty right from his birth. It is not surprising, therefore, that he exhibited excellent rulership qualities and was able to raise the Agaie Emirate to great and enviable levels during his reign.

His remarkable leadership qualities led to his being admired by all and sundry including the ruling houses of other Nupe Emirates including those of Bida, Lapai, Patigi, Lafiagi, Kontagora and others. It is in this context that other Nupe Emirates, notably Bida and Lapai, joined forces with him in joint military expeditions for the progress of the Nupe Nation as a whole.

It was Etsu Muhammadu Dikko who built and expanded Agaie town into a befitting palace. He built gigantic city walls round Agaie and welcome an exodus of many people from Bida into the town.

But Agaie became such a regaled and marvellous town to behold that the ever mischievous Etsu Masaba of Bida, out of jealousy and envy, invaded and destroyed many of the farmlands of Agaie in a blatant attempt to reduce the glory of Agaie.

In those days Etsu Masaba had become the most powerful man not only in KinNupe but throughout the Nigerian Middle Belt and Southern Nigeria. Through his endless expansionist wars he was able to build the Bida Emirate into the most powerful emirate in the whole of pre-Colonial Nigeria. Professor Smalldone actually documented the fact that in the days of Etsu Masaba the Great the Bida Emirate was the greatest military power in Nigeria.

When Etsu Masaba realized that he was the most powerful man of all his contemporaries, he decided to conquer all other neighbouring Nupe emirates into the fold of the Bida Emirate. He started by declaring that his sovereignty over both Lapai and Agaie emirates. But the Agaie Emirate was too big and powerful for him to just conquer like that.

First Etsu Muhammadu Dikko of Agaie asked Umaru Nagwamatse of Kontagora, who was also a cousin brother to Etsu Masaba, to help him against Masaba's aggression. In those days Umaru Nagwamatse was actually residing at Agaie, that was fater he was prevented from attacking the Abuja (now Suleja) Emirate by the Sultan of Sokoto. Umaru Nagwamatse then threatened to invade and burn Bida farms if Masaba didn't stop ravaging Agaie farmlands. Masaba subsequently stopped his wanton destruction of Agaie farmlands. Umaru Nagwamatse was known to be a stubborn and warlike prince in those days and Etsu Masaba of Bida knew that Umaru Bahaushe can cause him some little trouble even though the Bida military machinery was too powerful for Umaru Bahaushe. But, and besides, Etsu Masaba was not interested in fighting his cousin brother Umaru Bahaushe. Etsu Masaba therefore withdrew his forces from his earlier attack on Agaie territories.

But then some Agaie princes and warlords embarked on retaliatory destruction of farmlands belonging to farmers on the outskirts of the Bida Emirate. This led to hostilities between the two Emirates and almost led to a total declaration of war by Bida on the Agaie marauders.

In the end the Emir of Gwandu had to come and mediate a settlement between the Bida and Agaie Emirates. That was in the year 1871. The Emir of Gwandu came and demarketed the borders of the various Nupe Emirates including the borders of the Bida, Agaie, Lafiagi, Lapai, Tsaragi and Tsonga. This clearcut demarcation of the borders of of each of these Nupe emirates was a direct and deliberate check on the expansionist and powermongering machinations of Etsu Masaba the Great. It was obvious to Etsu Masaba that all the other Nupe emirs have connived with the Emir of Gwandu against him Etsu Masaba. This greatly angered and disillusioned Etsu Masaba who henceforth became very bitter against the Emir of Gwandu.

Etsu Masaba the Great of Bida died the folloing year 1872 at Bida.

After the death of Etsu Masaba the Great the Agaie Emirate, under Etsu Muhammadu Dikko, was able to continue with its peaceful development and sociocultural development without any trouble from the meddlesome rulers of Bida. But then diplomatic relations between Bida and Agaie were at there all-time low during that period.

The marvellous Etsu Muhammadu Dikko of Agaie died in 1877.

Prince Nuhu was turbaned in 1877 as the new Etsu of Agaie. When Etsu Nuhu of Agaie came to power things were such that the relationship between the Bida and the Agaie Emirates was still sour. So, Etsu Nuhu of Agaie and Etsu Umaru Majigi, who succeeded Masaba, were not that friendly towards one another.

But all the same, and faced with a common enemy in the form of the British imperialists, Etsu Nuhu of Agaie joined forces with the Bida rulers to repel the British forces under the Royal Niger Company. It is in this regard that Etsu Nuhu actually sent his army to help the Bida forces against the British forces in the Battle of Bida in 1897.

But on the first day of the Battle of Bida the Agaie forces sent to assist the Bida forces suffered a fatal defeat in the hands of the British RNC forces. Kpotun Buhari of Agaie, who was heading the Agaie forces, was killed together with many of his warriors from Agaie. This unfortunate incident was so devastating to the Agaie forces that immediately left the battleground and retreated back to Agaie that very day.

In any case the British forces of the Royal Niger Company conquered Bida the next day and, afterwards, they turned their attention on conquering Agaie too.

Two months later Etsu Nuhu of Agaie and his people fled Agaie town when the British forces invaded Agaie. Etsu Nuhu went and settled at Dakpan, accordingly known today as Etsugaie, as the Royal Niger Forces besieged Agaie for forty solid days. The name of Dakpan was changed to Etsugaie in memory of the fact that the Etsu Nuhu of Agaie, on flight from the devilish White men, sojourned at Dakpan for a while.

Later on Etsu Nuhu fled further from Dakpan to Tswachiko when he learnt that another contingent of the Royal Niger Company had invaded Lapai and that the Etsu of Lapai had also fled Lapai.

Etsu Nuhu came back to Agaie after the British forces left Agaie. Etsu Nuhu died in 1900.

Abubakar I was turbaned as the new Etsu of Agaie in 1900.

Because of the unfortunate experience of his predecessor, Etsu Abubakar I did not get himself involved in the Bida crisis when Etsu Bubakar of Bida went back to Bida in 1900 and ousted Etsu Muhammadu Makun, an act which prompted the Royal Niger Company forces to reinvade Bida again.

Yet, and on flight, Etsu Bubakar of Bida came and sojourned at Agaie. This attracted the Royal Niger Company forces to Agaie who invaded Agaie the next morning. By that time Etsu Bubakar had already left Agaie but the people of Agaie, including Etsu Abubakar I of Agaie, all fled Agaie when they saw the British forces of the Royal Niger Company.

Etsu Abubakar I came back to Agaie later when the Royal Niger Company forces left Agaie. After all these crises, Etsu Abubakar I was able to settle down and administered his Agaie Emirate in a most capable manner. He, however, had to accept and recognise British colonial sovereignty. He is considered as one of the most respected rulers of Agaie. He was indeed a great leader by all standards. Etsu Abubakar I died in 1919.

Abubakar II was turbaned as the new Etsu of Agaie in 1919. Etsu Abubakar II was the first Etsu of Agaie to be officially turbaned and installed by the British Colonial Government of Nigeria. His being on very good terms with the White colonialists enabled him to shift the Divisional Office from Baro to Agaie in 1920.

Etsu Abubakar II died in 1926. He is still remembered for his patriotic activities in favour of Agaie. Among many other such remarkable achievements he was the one who established a modern market at Agaie.

Abdullahi II was turbaned as the new Etsu of Agaie in 1926. He was one of the wealthiest of the Emirs of Agaie in modern historic times. He was also said to be a very powerful and very influential ruler. Etsu Abdullahi died in 1936.

Etsu Aliyu was turbaned as the new Etsu of Agaie in 1936. He was the first Western educated Etsu of Agaie. He attended the Kano Provincial School. Before becoming the Etsu of Agaie he extensive experience in rulership as he was the supervisor of the village heads of the Agaie Emirate for a number of years. With is Western education and royal experience backgrounds he was able to rule in a most remarkable manner when he became the Etsu of Agaie.

Etsu Aliyu was also the first Etsu of Agaie to go to Mecca for the Hajj pilgrimage in 1950. This was around the same time that the Etsu Nupe, Etsu Bakudu of Bida, also became the first Etsu Nupe to perform the Hajj pilgrimage to Mecca.

Etsu Aliyu died in 1953.

Muhammadu Bello was turbaned in 1953 as the new Etsu of Agaie. By the time of the turbaning of Etsu Muhammadu Bello the Colonial Government was already long in power, in fact there were already talks of Self Rule and the granting of Independence to Nigerians. It is no wonder, therefore, that the Agaie Native Authority played a key role in his turbaning as the new Etsu Agaie.

Etsu Muhammadu Bello is the longest reigning Etsu of Agaie on record. He reigned as the Etsu Agaie for 36 good years, from that 1953 till his death in 1989. He contributed a lot to the development and modernisation of the Agaie Emirate. Etsu Muhammadu Bello died in 1989.

Muhammadu Attahiru was turbaned as the new Etsu of Agaie in 1989. He was, however, dethroned five years later, in 1994, because he was accused of complicity in the murder of a chairman of the Agaie Local Government Area.

For some two or so years the Agaie Emirate throne remained vacant until Abubakar III was turbaned as the new Etsu Agaie in 1996. But this Etsu Abubakar III died less than two years into his reign in 1998.

For a year or so again the Agaie Emirate throne remained vacant as the dethroned Etsu Muhammadu Attahiru was in court trying to prove his innocence with regard to the case of the murdered chairman. In the end Etsu Attahiru won the case as he was able to prove that he had nothing to do with the murder of the chairman.

Etsu Muhammadu Attahiru was, accordingly, reinstated, for his second term, as the Etsu Agaie in 1999. During his second term he worked on the rebuilding of the Etsu Nuhu Mosque. He reigned as the Etsu Agaie for the second time till his death in 2003.

In 2003 Alhaji Muhammadu Kudu Abubakar III was turbaned as the new Etsu Agaie. He spent ten years in power as one of the most enlightened Etsu Nupes of modern times. He was a highly educated and a seasoned civil servant and a scientist at the same time. He was also one of the main champions of the Edu State Movement which is a movement dear to his subjects and the Nupe masses in general.

Etsu Muhammadu Kudu Abubakar III died on Sunday the 30th of March 2014. He was succeeded by Etsu Yusuf Nuhu who is the current Emir of Agaie.

BIDA

Bida is a very ancient settlement. Nobody knows for real when the settlement of Bida was first established. What is known for sure though is that it was the valleys and the rivers of the Landzun River that attracted the first settlers of Bida to their established on the banks of the river.

The Rivers of Bida

It also seems that Bida was originally not a single settlement but actually a cluster of ancient hamlets and villages closely-netted on the banks of the Landzun River.

In those earlier days the Landzun River was of course not the small and diminishing network of streams that we see it is today. In those days the Landzun was a big river with a network of streams and tributaries that came to serve the cluster of villages that eventually merged to form the Bida settlement. There was also a prominent Cikan River in those days aside from the Landzun River.

The Bini and Zhitakoro Merger

They said the various villages initially have their own separate names until they eventually merged into the single settlement that came to be identifies as Bida.

Bida was at the beginning a population of an ancient Bini Nupe people. At an earlier time in the ancient history of KinNupe the Bini people have migrated down from the northeast, from north-central Nigeria and across the Benue river and its confluence with the Niger to their final settlement on the banks of the River in Central KinNupe – a final location they still occupy to this very day.

But before the arrival of the Binis in Central KinNupe there were the Zhitakoro, with their almighty AtaGara Kingdom, occupying Central KinNupe. It was the Binis who came and displaced and drove the Zhitakoros out of Central KinNupe to their present location as the Dibos and the Gbagyis in south-eastern KinNupe and the FCT and the FCT and Kogi states.

But the Zhitakoro population was not completely wiped out of Central KinNupe. It is true that quite a larger section of the Zhitakoro population migrated out of Central KinNupe upon the collapse and fall of their AtaGara empire but a significant population of these Zhitakoro people did remained in Central KinNupe.

As the settler Bini people arrived KinNupe they began to mix and acculturate with the remaining Zhitakoro population that did not migrate out of KinNupe upon the fall of the AtaGara empire.

Bidako

The Bini and the Zhitakoro begun to mix and intermarry. In the end a new population of the Bini-Zhitakoro people emerged as synthesis of the settler Binis and the indigenous Zhitakoro people.

This Bini-Zhitakoro people were also referred to as the Bini-Zhitako or as the Bi-Tako or Bitako, as it survived into history to this very day, Bidako.

Bidako was the national name of the people that resulted from the assimilation of the settler Bini people into the indigenous population of the ancient Zhitakoro or Zhitako (the Dibo, Kyadya, Kakanda, etc, etc of modern times).

Bidako became a United Kingdom of the Bini and the AtaGara people long after the fall and demise of the ancient AtaGara empire of Central KinNupe.

But this Bidako was not a vibrant or excessively warlike kingdom as its predecessor AtaGara was. In fact Bidako was merely a nation of riverine canoe men navigating and fishing on the creeks and streams of the River Niger and its tributaries and effluences one of which was the Landzun River.

Bidako

On the banks and valleys of the Landzun River a population of these Bidako people clustered to form the Bidako settlement that became known to us today simply as Bida.

Of course the modern name Bida is merely a shortened form of the more ancient and more pristine name Bidako.

But Bida was also the name of the chief of the Bini people who built a walled fortification in the midst of the Bidako villages that clustered on the banks of the River Niger.

The story is that at a time a leading chief of the Bidako people on the banks of the Landzun built a wall round the central one among the cluster of Bidako villages on the banks of the Landzun. This walled village became known as the Banin Bida since the chief was styled the Nda Bida or, simply, as Bida himself.

And that was how we came about the small but walled ancient Bini village of Bida which simply remained as such on the banks of the Landzun for a long time unnoticed until the forces of history suddenly flung it unto the limelight of historical events in the latter half of the nineteenth century.

The Dendo Dynasts

Mallam Dendo arrived KinNupe at the beginning of the first half of the nineteenth century and by the middle of the nineteenth century his descendants have established the Dendo dynasty that have variously taken over Raba and Lade as their regional capital cities.

Actually the choice capital city was Raba which the Dendo dynasts have taken over from the Tsoede dynasts with Usman Zaki as the first Emir of the Dendo dynasty with Raba as his capital city.

Umaru Bahaushe and Bida

But Usman Zaki's restless and rebellious junior brother, Masaba, will just not let things be peacefully in the Nupe Nation. Masaba provoked Usman Zaki and Etsu Tsado one against the other and then sided with Etsu Tsado to sack and raze Raba to ashes in the disastrous Battle of Raba from which Usman Zaki escaped death in the whiskers.

Usman Zaki fled to Gwandu and Masaba declared himself the new Emir of Nupe with his capital city at Lade. But Masaba had hardly settle down to consolidate his rulership barely two years later when he was himself violently and disgracefully ousted from power by his own War General Umaru Bahaushe.

Umaru Bahaushe chased Masaba out of KinNupe and declared himself the new Emir of Nupe. And for nine solid years Umaru Bahaushe ruled over KinNupe with undisputable powers.

However, Umaru Majigi, the son of Mamman Majigi the first son of Mallam Dendo, came back from Gwandu to engage Umaru Bahaushe in a series of battles that eventually saw the young prince Umaru Majigi being pursued along the length and breadth of KinNupe by the far more experienced General Umaru Bahaushe whose gargantuan army was, in any case, far too great for the ragtag collection of mercenaries that the foolhardy Prince Umaru Majigi have marshalled.

General Umaru Bahaushe chased the Prince Umaru Majigi around until the prince took refuge in the small but walled Bini village of Bidako or Bida on the banks of the Landzu River.

General Umaru Bahaushe besieged the walled Bini village and waited patiently for hunger and starvation to force the young Prince Umaru Majigi into surrender.

Luck, however, ran out for General Umaru Majigi when, as he waited on the walls of Bida, different armies from different directions under the various Etsu Nupes and various Nupe Emir contenders – including Usman Zaki from Gwandu and Masaba from Ilorin – suddenly marched on Umaru Bahaushe's army.

General Umaru Bahaushe got drowned in the Gbako River while trying to flee the various armies concentrating on him from all directions.

Usman Zaki and Bida

After the death Umaru Bahaushe all the power stakeholders of KinNupe convened a second Raba Convention in the year 1856. At this Second Raba Convention, attended by the Emir Halilu of Gwandu, it was unanimously agreed that Usman Zaki be allowed his Second Term as the Emir of Nupe. Thus was Usman Zaki reinstalled for his Second Term as the Emir of Nupe.

And it was unanimously agreed at this Second Raba Convention that Etsu Isa should be recognised as the legitimate and paramount Etsu Nupe of the entire Nupe Nation. The condition of Etsu Isa was, however, a token and ceremonial one actually.

First the office of the Emir of Nupe, occupied by Usman Zaki, have by then completely overshadowed the office of the Etsu Nupe, now occupied by Etsu Isa, which have been rendered completely obsolete.

Secondly, even though the Fulani Dendo dynasts claimed to have recognised Etsu Isa as the paramount Etsu Nupe of the entire Nupe Nation, they still held him captive as a prisoner of war. Imagine a prisoner-of-war Etsu Nupe.

In any case it was also unanimously agreed at this Second Raba Convention that Masaba should be the turbaned as the Sarkin Fulani.

And Umaru Majigi was unanimously turbaned as the Yerima to Usman Zaki.

Interestingly enough the new Emir Usman Zaki decided to chose Bida as his new capital city. His reasons for shifting the capital city of Nupe from Raba to Bida are many and variegated.

Usman Zaki's first reason for choosing Bida as the new capital city is that Raba have been razed to ashes beyond repair during the disastrous Battle of Raba in 1841.

Then Usman Zaki also chose Bida because of the strategic location of Bida in the valleys of the Landzun River in such a manner that a massive and sudden attack along the River Niger upon Bida is impossible – the unfortunate fate that destroyed Raba.

And it was quite safer, from security perspectives, to start a new capital city all over again away from the court machinations and perennial palace coups that have became the hallmark of royal life at Raba over the decades.

In any case Usman Zaki simply remained at Bida with the gargantuan conglomeration of armies that have transformed the erstwhile small, but walled, Bini village of Bida into a massive war camp during the sustained campaign against the late General Umaru Bahaushe of, as the Dendo Dynasts now claim, usurper memories.

Usman Zaki laid out a master-plan for the town-planning design of Bida as the most befitting capital city in the whole of the West African sub-region. The streets and boulevards of the new capital city were planned and designed in such a manner that more than half a century later Professor Leo Frobenius could still rate Bida as the greatest city in the whole of the Central Sudan.

Unfortunately Usman Zaki died in 1859 only three years into his Second Term as the Emir of Nupe and, that, at the height of his building Bida into the greatest capital city in the whole of the Central Sudan.

Etsu Masaba and Bida

Masaba became the next Emir of Nupe and he retained Bida as the new capital of Nupe. Masaba's expansionist and commercialist style of rulership immediately transformed Nupe into far a greater economic power that instantaneously attracted massive and untold wealth and infrastructural development to Bida the capital city.

And, Masaba's lengthy Second Term, for fourteen prosperous years, from that 1859 to 1873, saw the transformation of Bida into the Splendour of the Central Sudan.

So prosperous and prestigious became Bida that it, incredibly enough, became the envy of other Nupe-Fulani emirates including those of Agaie and Lapai which led to serious clashes between Masaba and the rulers of Agaie and Lapai.

Bida became the commercial and economic headquarters of the Central Sudan to such and extent that the British have to send a trade high commissioner, in the person of W.H. Simpson, to be permanently stationed at Bida to oversee and protect the gargantuan volume of commercial and trading activities that became the norm between the British and Bida from that time of Etsu Masaba onward.

The warlike Masaba also transformed Bida into the military superpower of the entire Central Sudan. In the days of Masaba there was no any other emirate, kingdom or power in the whole of the Central Sudan that had the military power of the Bida Emirate. Bida was the singular military superpower of the Central Sudan in those days. Even the entire Sokoto Caliphate complex was wholly dependent on the Bida Emirate for its economic and military integrity.

Masaba died in 1873 and was succeeded by Umaru Majigi as the new Emir of Nupe.

Etsu Umaru Majigi and Bida

By the time Umaru Majigi became the Emir of Nupe Bida was already a great capital city rivalling many other great capital cities in the Central Sudan. But Umaru Majigi had this unparalleled passion for the transformation of Bida into a greater capital city.

It was Umaru Majigi who deliberately decided to give excessive attention to the perfection of the three royal palaces that bedecked Bida as among the Great Wonders of the Central Sudan to this very day. It was also Umaru Majigi who expanded and built the Great Night Market for which Bida became famous throughout the West African sub-region.

The point here is that Umaru Majigi became the Emir of the Nupe Nation at a time when Bida have, as a capital city of Nupe, already accumulated enough wealth, power and fame to have raised it unto the pedestals of the greatest power in the whole of the Central Sudan. This fact is illustrated, for instance, by the incident that it was to this same Umaru Majigi, as the Emir of Nupe, that the Emir of Gwandu came seeking for assistance against the Giro rebels who almost brought the Sokoto Caliphate to an untimely end in the early 1880s.

It was the Bida forces under Umaru Majigi who went up north and conquered the Giro rebels, thereby saving the Sokoto Caliphate. The Sokoto Caliphate had become, in reality, a dependency of the superpower Bida Emirate.

So great did Bida become in those days that rebellions against its widespread sovereignty began to increase. In just the eleven or so years of Emir Umaru Majigi he had to contend with many rebellions two of which were the cataclysmic rebellions of the Efa Gbagba rebellion of 1876 by Etsu Baba and the 1882 Ganigan Rebellion of the Kyadyas.

Emir Umaru Majigi died in 1882 after successfully building Bida into the most beautiful and most powerful capital city in the whole of West Africa.

Etsu Maliki and Bida

That very year 1882 Etsu Maliki was immediately turbaned as the new Emir of Nupe after the death of Umaru Majigi.

Etsu Maliki came to power at a time when Bida was the greatest, largest and richest city in sub-Saharan Africa. In fact Etsu Maliki, on the authority of Professor S.F. Nadel, became the richest Etsu Nupe and hence the richest man in Black Africa in those days.

And Etsu Maliki was so ambitious about building Bida into a greater city. Etsu Maliki was more or a intellectual and an Islamic scholar and wasn't that warlike but he was surrounded by his zealously war generals including Mayaki Ndajiya, Shaba Mamudu and Abdulkadiri. These people helped Etsu Maliki in brigning the Ganigan War to an end. They also helped Etsu Maliki in arresting and executing the leaders of the Kyadya people who initiated the Ganigan War against Bida with the aim of bringing Bida and the Dendo dynasts to an end ever since the days of Etsu Umaru Majigi.

Etsu Maliki also attacked, subdued and almost destroyed the Lafiagi and Tsonga emirates because he accused the royalties of these two emirates of siding with the rebellious Kyadya and, together with Sierra Leonian merchants, of providing the Kyadya rebels with the weapons which they used to fight the Ganigan War against Bida and the Dendo dynasts. Etsu Maliki imposed the infamous Ajele taxation system on Lafiagi and Tsonga as a punishment.

Etsu Maliki also extended and expanded Nupe territory into a significant section of Yorubaland using the southern Nupe emirates of Lafiagi, Tsonga and Tsaragi as his war launchpads. A large section of the Yorubas became a subject people to the Nupes all over again.

Etsu Maliki also firm up the power and sovereignty of Bida by increasing the population of the Bida Emirate through the establishment of almost 400 new villages, or tungazhi, in various parts of KinNupe. Professor Michael Mason discussed this in exhaustive detailed when he talked about the clientale serfdom system used by the Etsu Nupe to resettle prisoners of war and other displaced populations brought into KinNUpe to concentrate the population of KinNupe by the Etsu Nupes.

With these war success story and experience Etsu Maliki was able to further consolidate the power and reputation of Bida as an indomitable and almighty superpower in the Central Suda, that is, ancient Nigeria and its neighbouring country. Bida became the military powerhouse of the entire Central Sudan and every city state, nation or people in ancient West Africa feared Bida and dreaded the Nupe people.

Towards the end of the reign of Etsu Maliki the pernicious and imperialist influence of the British gradually became a menace to the Nupe Nation which was the only superpower that the British saw as a real threat in the whole of the Central Sudan. Etsu Maliki was completely opposed to the imperialist and colonialist designs of the mischievous and double-speaking White men.

Etsu Maliki died in 1895 and was succeeded by Etsu Bubakar as the new Etsu Nupe.

Etsu Bubakar and Bida

But Etsu Bubakar was even more opposed to the devilish White men colonialists and it is no wonder that just some two years into his reign as the new Etsu Nupe, that is in 1897, the British viciously attacked the very city of Bida in what is today known to historians as the Battle of Bida.

The British deposed Etsu Bubakar, he actually fled Bida in the face of the invading British army; the British then installed the more pliable Etsu Makun in the stead of Etsu Bubakar.

But the moment the British left the people of Bida ousted Makun from power and reinstalled Etsu Bubakar as their legitimate Etsu Nupe. The Royal Niger Forces, calling itself the RWAFF under Frederick Lugard the Anti-Nupe, came back and re-depose Etsu Bubakar again and reinstalled Etsu Makun again. This time around the British forces forcibly banished Etsu Bubakar to Lokoja where his was to spent the rest of his life and where his tomb can be seen to this very day.

In all these crises Bida as a polity and as a metropolis rapidly deteriorated from being a great and famous capital city to being a degenerate and fallen ghost town from which all and sundry fled. To this very day Bida has never truly regained its lost glory ever since those bleak 1897 days.

From that year 1897 to 1901 Bida was reduced to an unfortunate state of anarchy and utter confusion all due in no small measure to the machinations of the British colonialists who were simply out to use their infamous divide et imperia scheme on the Nupe Nation.

The British played the Nupe royalty one against the other – in particular they set up the overambitious Makun against Etsu Bubakar on the one hand inside the Bida polity and then, outside Bida they mobilised the ancient Kyadya and Yisa Nupe peoples against the Bida Emirate.

The defeat of Bida at the Battle of Bida was brought about and effected by the British through this two-pronged approach: first they succeeded in retaining the Bida army with Makun at Ogidi somewhere in today's Kogi State then they also mobilised the Kyadya leaders from supporting the Bida authorities against the British forces at the right psychological moment in the peak of the battle between the RWAFF and the Bida forces.

In any case Bida was bombarded by the Maxim Gun, the first machine gun in history, purposefully and custom designed in the war foundries of England for the war with Bida. The advanced military weaponry and the internal and external dissensions and betrayals by variously provoked factions led to the wholesale defeat of the Bida forces under Etsu Bubakar.

Etsu Bubakar fled Bida and the British forces came in and install Makun as the new Emir of Bida. Etsu Muhammadu Makun thus became the first White man appointed Emir of Bida.

But when the Bristish left Etsu Bubakar came back, deposed Etsu Makun and drove him out of Bida. However, the British came back, chased Etsu Bubakar out of Bida, then recalled and re-installed Etsu Makun as the new Emir of Bida.

Etsu Muhammadu Makun and Bida

By the time Frederick Lugard the Anti-Nupe had reinstalled Etsu Makun as the new Etsu Nupe the Colonial Government have already been established and Bida became an unwilling 'dependency' or 'protectorate' of the British Government. This way Frederick Lugard, who became the First Governor General of the New Government, was able to use all the administrative and colonial powers at his disposal to destroy Bida and reduce the Nupe Nation into a joke of its glorious past.

Etsu Idirisu who was a prisoner under the Dendo dynasts in Bida was freed by the British and was assisted by the British to establish a new emirate, Patigi Emirate, for the Jimada section of the Tsoede dynasty, at Patigi just across the banks of the River Niger.

Etsu Kolo Yisa, of the Majiya section of the Tsoede dynasty, went and establish himself as the new Etsu Nupe at Zugurma with the indirect support of the White men colonialists.

The Colonialists also excised the Yagba, Kakanda, Bassa and Bunu people from the servitude to the Bida Emirate and ensure full independence from the overall Nupe Nation for these various people who are actually Nupes themselves.

All these were deliberate machinations by the White men colonialists to balkanize and weaken the Nupe Nation in general and the Bida Emirate in particular. As the late Professor Idris Abdullahi painfully demonstrated, the Nupe

Nation, and the Bida Emirate in particular, was deliberately and mischievously balkanised into puny polities and districts.

But Etsu Muhammadu Makun tried his best in developing Bida under British rule. It was during his reign that the Native Authority of British rule was established in Bida and, to be fair to Etsu Makun, this brought about a lot of development along modern lines to Bida.

In any case Etsu Makun died in 1916 and was immediately succeeded by Etsu Muhammadu Bello as the new Etsu Nupe.

Etsu Muhammadu Bello and Bida

By the time of Etsu Bello Bida was already and totally prostrated before the bloody talons of the British Colonial Government and it is no wonder, therefore, that under the reign of Etsu Bello there was an influx of European traders and expatriates who came and set up commercial and trading posts all over Bida metropolis.

Etsu Bello was himself a businessman and he actually became very wealthy. He was the first Nupe man to own a car and many other Nupencizhi became owners of cars during his time. Etsu Bello thus ensured that roads are constructed throughout the length and breadth of the Bida Emirate.

Etsu Bello was also a great leader who greatly helped the masses and brought the benefit of rulership to the grassroots level. He thus became very popular among the masses.

Etsu Bello reigned for ten years until his death in 1926.

Etsu Saidu Mamudu and Bida

Etsu Muhammadu Bello was succeeded by Etsu Saidu as the new Etsu Nupe in 1926. Etsu Saidu was said to be a pious, Islamic-minded, Etsu Nupe who was able to institute some Islamic reformations in the administrative system of the Bida Emirate.

Etsu Saidu was the first to lay the foundations of the first three-arms zone in Nigeria. The Wadata Palace, Secretariat and Court that are still there for all to see in Wadata, Bida, were first established by Etsu Saidu with the assiatnce of the Colonial Government.

Etsu Saidu died in 1935.

Etsu Bakudu

Etsu Muhammadu Ndayako, popularly known as Etsu Bakudu, became the new Etsu Nupe after Etsu Saidu.

Etsu Bakudu was one of the most remarkable Etsu Nupes in modern Nupe history. Despite the debilitating handicap of having to rule under Colonial domination he was able to significantly develop the Bida Emirate and to move the Nupe Nation forward in a modernistic manner.

Etsu Bakudu was a popular Etsu Nupe well loved by the masses as he took all the time to personally interact with and honour the masses and the lay people. He was the first Etsu Nupe to started giving royal titles to eminent Nupe people who are not members of the royal families and he recruited these titled non-royal Nupencizhi in his cabinet council.

He also used to personally toured the Bida Emirate and sit down with villagers and other townspeople in all the nooks and corner of the Bida Emirate in order to discuss with them and know their problems and plights.

He personally visited both Lagos and London in order to appraise himself of the nature of the modern world. He was the first Etsu Nupe to sit and personally discuss with the Queen of England. He was also the first, and so far only, sitting Etsu Nupe to write a book. He wrote a book titled 'Njin Etsu Nupe'.

Etsu Bakudu was able to bring a lot of modern educational developmental, infrastructural developments into the various aspects and facets of the Bida Emirate. He also witnessed the Independence of Nigeria from the British.

Etsu Bakudu died in 1962.

Etsu Usman Sarki

Etsu Bakudu was succeeded by Etsu Usman Sarki. Etsu Usman Sarki was a highly charismatic, intellectually-minded, sophisticated but controversial figure.

Etsu Usman Sarki was the first Etsu Nupe to acquire Western education and he was, by the standards of those days, a highly educated individual. He in fact rose to the enviable position of a Federal Minister in the Federal Civil Service before he became the Etsu Nupe.

Etsu Usman Sarki had all the energy and charisma to move the Nupe Nation forward, and was indeed capably doing so, when he was controvertibly dethroned due to a lot of allegations of misrule against him in 1969.

Etsu Bello

Etsu Musa Bello became the new Etsu Nupe in 1969 after the deposition of the controversial Etsu Usman Sarki. Etsu Musa Bello had a peaceful and relatively prosperous reign until he died seven years later in 1975.

Etsu Umaru Sanda

Etsu Musa Bello was succeeded by Etsu Umaru Sanda in 1975 as the new Etsu Nupe.

Etsu Umaru Sanda had a prosperous and lengthy reign that lasted for twenty-eight solid years from that 1975 up to his death in the year 2003.

The reigning Etsu Yahaya Abubakar became the new Etsu Nupe in 2003 after the death of Etsu Umaru Sanda.

LAFIAGI

Origin of the Name 'Lafiagi'.

In former times KinNupe was known as Ife, Ifa or Apa. It is this ancient national name of KinNupe that is still known as Apa among the Idoma, Igbira, Igala and many other ancient Nigerian peoples who originated from and left KinNupe in those days when KinNupe was still known as Apa.

It is this same ancient national name of KinNupe that is still known as Ife, Ile Ife or Ifa among the ancient Yoruba people who originated from and left KinNupe in those days when KinNupe was still known as Elemkpe, Ele Ife, Ife or Ifa.

Apa was also pronounced as Apai or Pai. And, accordingly, KinNupe was also known in ancient times as Pai.

In those days most of the rivers that pass through KinNupe – including the River Niger and any of its tributaries – were generally referred to as La-Pai or Lapai. The prefix 'la' in this case being a latter form of the ancient 'ra' which was the original Nupe word for 'a body of water' such that 'Ra-Pai' or 'La-Pai' will simply and directly mean the 'Water of Pai' or the 'River of Pai-Land', that is, and as we might translate it today, 'The River of Nupeland'.

It was this ancient Nupe word, 'Lapai' that was generically applied to all the rivers in KinNupe in very ancient times.

But then the very name 'Lapai' itself has an endless variety of dialectal variants and synonyms. Lapai was also variously pronounced as Lafai, Lafia or, as we pronounce it today, Lafiagi.

Actually the variant 'Lafia' was popularised by the loaning of the Hausa 'Lafia', which is itself a corruption of the Arabic 'Khafiya' or 'healthy', into Nupe.

Lafiagi the Original Ile Ife
In those days all the rivers in KinNupe were variously known as Lapai, Lafia or Lafiagi. With time all riverine settlements in KinNupe also became generally identified as Lapai, Lafia or Lafiagi. Actually Lapai, Lafia or Lafiagi was originally used as a place marker as in, for instance, 'Lafiagi Katsa' or the 'Lafiagi of katsa' which will mean 'The Riverine Settlement of Katsa'.

That was how we came about the present town of Lafiagi in Edu Local Government of Kwara State – it used to be just one of the various Lafiagis, that is, Nupe riverine settlements. And it used to have its original, proper name apart from the generic Lafiagi riverine name.

But what was peculiar about this particular Lafiagi of today's Edu Local Government Area is that it was located right on the banks of the River Niger.

The point is that since it was located on the very banks of the River Niger it was evidently one of the original Ile Ifes mentioned in ancient Nupe and Yoruba traditions as being among the first of the earlier Ile Ifes.

The Odu Ifa Divination panegyrics of the Yoruba people categorically stated, to this very day, that the modern city of Ile Ife was not the original Ile Ife founded by Oduduwa or even Oramiyan.

Professor Obayemi demonstrated that modern Ile Ife is at least the eighth Ile Ife from the original Ile Ife which was located in KinNupe. Professor Lawal Babatunde also wrote that Original Ile Ife was a Nupe town located in KinNupe.

There were several original Ile Ife settlements in various parts of KinNupe before the eventual Ile Ife that we see in Osun State today was founded. In fact the Yoruba traditions of Oduduwa residing in Ile Ife were in reference to that original Ile Ife that was first founded and established in KinNupe and, accordingly, Oduduwa was a Nupe man.

Today's Lafiagi was evidently one of the original Nupe Ile Ifes "sitting on the River Niger" reported by the first European explorers and missionaries to arrive KinNupe. As late as the 1830s the Lander brothers were told at Old Oyo, by Yoruba people pointing towards today's Lafiagi, that original Ile Ife was a Nupe town located on the banks of the River Niger.

Reverend T.J. Bowen and G.O George, who were among the first Europeans to visit Yorubaland, also referred to Lafiagi as the original Ile Ife.

The point here, and as we pointed out right at the beginning of this article, is that the names 'Ife' and 'Ifa' and 'Fai' or 'Fia' are one and the same ancient names pronounced differently due to dialectal differences. It is therefore clear that 'Ile Ife' can also be pronounced as 'Ile Fia' or, simply, as 'Lefia' or as 'Lafia' which can then go to be pronounced as 'Lafiagi' as we do today.

Ancient Lafiagi

Whatever the case might have been it is obvious that many present-day Nupe settlements – including Fogbe, Tafian, Lapai, Lafiagi and Patigi – are among the original Ile Ifes mentioned in the ancient traditions of the Nupe and Yoruba peoples.

They said present-day Lafiagi used to be a very ancient village in the midst of surrounding villages on the banks of the River Niger. It was its location on the very banks of the River Niger that attracted travellers and passers-by to it as a place of sojourn whenever they are crossing the River Niger.

Actually Lafiagi and its collection of neighbouring villages form a port of entry through the River Niger to the trans-Niger half of KinNupe in those ancient days. Lafiagi was also an important port of call on the route of ancient caravan and trade route that linked the southern half of ancient Central Sudan, that is ancient Nigeria and its neighbours, with its northern half.

So, Lafiagi has always been there as a very ancient port of the River Niger. And nobody can really tell when Lafiagi was first founded as a settlement on the very banks of the River Niger in those very far off days.

But then, and particularly in the latter half of the seventeenth century, KinNupe became the headquarters of a Central Sudan-wide Islamic Revolution due to the fervent desire on the part of the Etsu Nupes in those days to set up an Islamic Caliphate to replace the declining power of the then Songhai empire.

That was how KinNupe became a centripetal magnate attracting Muslim Jihadists and itinerant nomads and pastoralists from all parts of the Central Sudan and even beyond.

That was how many Mallams, including Mallam Dendo, Mallam Alimi, Man Musa Kodogi, Mallam Sharif Balarabe and many other Mallams came and settled in different parts of KinNupe at the end of the eighteenth century and the beginning of the nineteenth centuries.

Mallam Dendo and Etsu Zubairu Majiya II

Mallam Dendo arrive KinNupe in the very first decade of the nineteenth century. He was warmly welcomed by the Etsu Nupes and eventually settled down at the Zugurma and Raba palaces of Etsu Zubairu Majiya II.

Mallam Dendo became a favourite of Etsu Zubairu Majiya II because of Mallam Dendo's fame for asiri magical prowess. Etsu Zubairu Majiya engaged the services of Mallam Dendo against his opponent Etsu Jimada who ruled over the Western half of the Nupe Nation with capital at Zugurma and Raba.

But then the fame and popularity of Mallam Dendo began to gradually overshadow that of Etsu Zubairu Majiya at Raba. Other Mallams from all parts of West Africa and beyond were trooping down to Raba to join the rapidly growing followership of Mallam Dendo at Raba.

Though slightly alarmed Etsu Zubairu Majiya didn't really mind the growing fame of Mallam Dendo at Raba until the incident of Mallam Alimi at Ilorin took place.

Mallam Alimi have also come into KinNupe in the same manner that Mallam Dendo came into KinNupe. But though Mallam Dendo had settled at Raba Mallam Alimi had settled at Ilorin.

Mallam Alimi had initially settled quietly and innocuously at Ilorin but his followership had suddenly exploded due to his fame as a Mallam with a lot of asiri talismanic powers. In the end the initially self-effacing Mallam Alimi became suddenly bold and assertive to the extent of waging Jihad wars and conquering Ilorin which he established into his own emirate.

Political observers immediately alerted Etsu Zubairu Majiya II to the possibility of Mallam Dendo re-enacting the same thing at Raba in KinNupe. That was when Etsu Zubairu Majiya became alarmed and decided to do something to curb the growing powers and threat of Mallam Dendo at Raba.

Etsu Zubairu Majiya II eventually drove Mallam Dendo out of Raba and declared a war of extermination against all the Mallams in KinNupe.

Well, Etsu Zubairu Majiya eventually came to see all these Mallams as constituting a threat to his sovereignty over KinNupe so he drove all the Mallams out of Central KinNupe.

The Battle Of Ilorin Or Mugba Mugba Battle
The Mallams from different parts of KinNupe went and regrouped under Mallam Alimi at Ilorin.

At Ilorin these Mallams, prominent among whom was Mallam Dendo, began to reach out to all possible helps from all directions. They begged Etsu Isa, also known as Etsu Idirisu, who was the son of the Etsu Jimada killed by Etsu Zubairu Majiya II at Ragada, to come and head and lead them at Ilorin against Etsu Zubairu Majiya II. They also called on all other Mallams and Islamic Jihadists from all parts of the Central Sudan to come to their aid against Etsu Zubairu Majiya whom they now labelled as a pagan Etsu Nupe intent on wiping out Islam from KinNupe.

Many Mallams, mercenaries and Jihadists from different parts of KinNupe did flock to and joined the Rebel Mallams at Ilorin.

Among those Mallams who joined the Rebel Mallams at Ilorin was one certain Mallam Maliki and his brother called Manzuma.

In any case Etsu Zubairu Majiya II suddenly attacked the Mallams at Ilorin with a gargantuan army of over 4,000 cavalry and over 1,000 infantry. It was a vicious and bloody war that was initially in favour of Etsu Zubairu Majiya's army. But in the end the battle miraculously turned against Etsu Majiya's gargantuan army. The victorious Mallam Dendo-Alimi mercenaries were to later come up with a tradition that Etsu Majiya II was defeated through the asiri charms of Mallam Dendo.

Whatever might have been the case Etsu Zubairu Majiya II was not only defeated but was also pursued across the Niger right back through Raba and thence unto Zugurma.

After the pursuit Mallam Dendo, on his way back, settled at Raba and begun to gradually built Raba into an emirate for his own filial dynasts.

Mallam Maliki Settled At Lafiagi

On return from the pursuit Mallam Maliki and his brother Manzuma crossed the River Niger but, instead of going thenceforth to Ilorin, he simply settled down on the River Niger port-town of Lafiagi with his brother Manzuma.

Mallam Maliki and his brother Manzuma chose the location of Lafiagi because it was located in the general area that was variously referred to as Ifa, Efa, Afa, Apa, Ofa, Ife, and so on and on.

They said that there used to be an ancient river, a tributary of the River Niger, which was known as Ifa or Ife and that this same river was the one that came to be known in latter times as Lafia or, as we call it today, Lafiagi.

Whatever the case might have been this ancient Lafia or Lafiagi was evidently one of the earlier Ife or Ile Ife areas referred to by the Odu Ifa as being one of the original sixteen Ile Ifes before the modern Ile Ife at Oyo State.

The initial aim of Mallam Maliki and his brother Manzuma was to quietly preach Islam among the neighbouring villages of Lafiagi.

In fact Mallam Maliki spent his time quietly teaching Islam and assisting the locals with his asiri charms. Together with Mallam Dendo at Raba, Mallam Maliki never actually thought of establishing a political emirate at Lafiagi. Just like Mallam Dendo at Raba, Mallam Maliki was content with the innocuous-sounding and obscure title of the 'Amir-ul-Muminin' of the Muslims in his immediate local surroundings.

And this is even though, and together with his brother Manzuma, Mallam Maliki began to build, somewhere around the year 1810, a fortified enclosure at Lafiagi in order to ward off future attacks similar to that of Etsu Zubairu Majiya II.

Mallam Maliki, however, died in 1824.

Emir Manzuma

After the death of Mallam Maliki his junior brother Manzuma was turbaned as the new, and first, Emir of Lafiagi. Mallam Maliki's son, called Aliyu, was too young to be turbaned as the First Emir of Lafiagi.

But a couple of years into the reign of Emir Manzuma, somewhere around the year 1830, Etsu Isa who helped the Rebel Mallams to crush Etsu Zubairu Majiya II at Ilorin, declared a war, in turn, against all the Mallams in KinNupe again.

At Edun, which Etsu Isa had chosen as his new capital city, Etsu Isa discovered a plot by the Mallams at his palace to overthrow him from power due to his young age and relative inexperience in rulership. He subsequently drove all the Mallams away from Edun and declared a war against all the Mallams in KinNupe.

The Mallams ran away to Raba where they rallied under the leadership of Mallam Dendo. Etsu Isa decided to march on Raba with the intention to put a final end to the Rebel Mallams in KinNupe.

But on his way to Raba Etsu Isa decided to sack any other town or city harbouring any Mallam and that was how he came upon Lafiagi and sacked the town. Emir Manzuma and his people fled to Ilorin in the face of Etsu Isa gargantuan army.

Etsu Isa completely destroyed and burnt down the old town of Lafiagi. Emir Manzuma and others narrowly escaped by the whiskers.

Etsu Isa then proceeded with his march on Raba. At Raba he laid siege on the city waiting for Mallam Dendo and the Rebel Mallams to capitulate. But luck later on ran out on Etsu Isa when Mallam Dendo was able to surreptitiously invited Etsu Zubairu Majiya II back to come and engage Etsu Isa on the walls of Raba.

Etsu Zubairu Majiya II, coming from exile in Agwara in Kambariland, mobilised an almighty army that immediately put the army of Etsu Isa to route. There was not really an engagement as the army of Etsu Isa retreated and fled back to

Edun in the face of the almighty army of Etsu Zubairu Majiya II.

From Edun Etsu Isa and his army were pursued further as the Rebel Mallams headed by Mallam Dendo joined forces with Etsu Zubairu Majiya II to attack Etsu Isa t Edun.

After the defeat and pursuit of Etsu Isa, Emir Manzuma was able to return from Ilorin to Lafiagi.

Upon his return from Ilorin Manzuma was now forced to form a stronger alliance with the Dendo dynasts at Raba. It was clear that his Nupe subjects of the newly created Lafiagi Emirate cannot be completely relied upon in times of trouble as is evidenced by the secret support some Lafiagi Nupes gave to Etsu Zubairu Majiya II when he sacked and burnt the town on his way to besiege Raba.

In those days many Nupe people of Lafiagi Emirate, especially from the surrounding villages, simply saw the Lafiagi Emirate dynasts of both the Maliki and Manzuma royalties, as people of Fulani descents and they therefore supported the Nupe Etsu Zubairu Majiya II against them.

To stem the tide of these problems Emir Manzuma was forced to accept Dendo hegemony over his Lafiagi Emirate. He was, for instance, coerced into appointing Ajele taxation and police officers over every district and settlement in his Lafiagi Emirate. But these Ajeles report more or less directly to Emir Usman Zaki at Raba who is their paramount employer.

After the death of Mallam Dendo in 1932 at Raba Usman Zaki became the paramount ruler of the Nupe Nation when his elder brother, Muhammadu Majigi, died a year into his position as the new Amir-ul-Muminin of KinNupe.

In his new position as the paramount ruler of KinNupe Emir Usman Zaki instituted a number of punitive measures against the Ndakpwatwa of Tsaragi. The Dendo dynasts have implicated the Ndakpwatwa and his Tsaragi Nupe subjects as supporters of both Etsu Zubairu Majiya II and Etsu Isa against the Fulanis and the Rebel Mallams in general when both declared their wars against the Rebel Mallams in 1806 and 1830 respectively.

First Emir Usman Zaki blatantly and mischievously declared and elevated the Olukpako head of the Igbominas of Share to a Nupe chieftaincy title that effectively removed the Olukpako from the authority of the Ndakpwatwa or Etsu of Tsaragi.

But, and more ignominious, was the manner in which Emir Usman Zaki imposed his Ajele taxation and police officers in every nook and corner of the entire Gudu Province that once belonged to the Ndakpwatwa or Etsu Tsaragi.

In fact the Dendo dynasts headed by Emir Usman Zaki at Raba blatantly divided and shared out the Gudu land of the Ndakpwatwa among their Fulani and Rebel Mallam fiefs. It is in this regard that Emir Usman Zaki cut the lands of today's Lafiagi and Patigi Emirates out of the Ndakpwatwa's Gudu Province and gave them out as fiefdoms to Emir Manzuma of Lafiagi.

All these, of course, greatly enhanced the power of Emir Manzuma and his Lafiagi Emirate.

But Emir Manzuma died around that very time in 1833.

Emir Aliyu of Lafiagi.

After the death of Emir Manzuma, Aliyu, the son of Mallam Maliki became the next, that is second, Emir of Lafiagi.

This Aliyu was the same who was too young to become the Emir upon the death of his father Mallam Maliki in 1824.

When Aliyu became a grown-up man, and with his uncle Manzuma as the Emir of Lafiagi, Aliyu went westward and founded the town of Tsonga whereby the royal dynasty of Tsonga originated.

Upon the death of his uncle Manzuma, Aliyu came back to Lafiagi and was turbaned as the next Emir of Lafiagi in 1833.

But Emir Aliyu had hardly settled down as the new Emir of Lafiagi when, in 1834, he immediately got embroiled in a terrible trouble beyond his control.

Masaba, the rebellious junior brother of Emir Usman Zaki, was banished by his elder brother from Raba. Masaba came down to seek asylum at Lafiagi but Emir Aliyu couldn't allow him settle at Lafiagi in order not to draw the ire of Emir Usman Zaki. Emir Aliyu instead allowed Masaba to take refuge at Lade.

But Masaba was so angered by this cold reception from Emir Aliyu that he, in his characteristic scheming manner, got the Emir of Gwandu and other Mallams to unanimously deposed Emir Aliyu from power as the Emir of Lafiagi.

Emir Aliyu was deposed as the Emir of Lafiagi in 1834 and was made to go back to being the ruler of Tsonga.

Emir Abdulkadir Manzuma

Upon the deposition of Emir Aliyu, Abdulkadir the son of the late Manzuma was immediately turbaned as the new, that is the third, Emir of Lafiagi.

But hardly have the new Emir Abdulkadir Manzuma settled down as the new Emir of Lafiagi than another big crisis broke out in the KinNupe of those days.

Etsu Zubairu Majiya II had died at that time in 1835 and his son, Tsado, was coroneted as the new Etsu Nupe.

Etsu Tsado, a remarkable figure in Nupe history, who is a direct descendant of the ancient Tsoede dynasty have refused to hand over the ancient Tsoede regalia of power to Emir Usman Zaki. Without those regalia Emir Usman Zaki was having a problem of legitimacy and credibility among the general Nupe populace who look upon as a mere Fulani usurper of Nupe rulership.

The ever rebellious and scheming Masaba have taken advantage of this rift between Etsu Tsado and Emir Usman Zaki and eventually succeeded in pitching the two against one another. The resulting series of battles ended in the woeful defeat of Emir Usman Zaki by Etsu Tsado.

In the last series of battles in 1841 Masaba have joined forces with Etsu Tsado and they besieged Raba. Emir Usman Zaki mysteriously escaped from Raba and in company of his nephew, Umaru Majigi, fled to Gwandu after sojourning at Agaie.

When Masaba and Etsu Tsado discovered that Emir Usman Zaki have escaped from Raba they attacked, sacked and burnt Raba to rubbles and ashes.

For the next couple of years afterwards KinNupe was in a state of chaos though Etsu Tsado became the paramount Etsu Nupe over the Nupe Nation at with his capital city at Gbara.

Masaba have also declared himself the new Emir of Nupe immediately after the battle of Raba. But supporters of the exiled Emir Usman Zaki will not recognise Masaba as the new Emir of Nupe.

In the end Emir Halilu of Gwandu summoned a convention of all the Etsu Nupes and all the Mallams at Raba. At that Raba Convention in 1845 Masaba was officially and unanimously recognised as the new Emir of Nupe. Emir Usman Zaki had to abdicate in favour of his brother Masaba in order to let peace reign.

At that same Raba Convention most of the land of the Lafiagi Emirate was taken away from Emir Abdulkadir Manzuma of Lafiagi and given over to the new Emir Masaba.

To make matters worse for Emir Abdulkadir Manzuma the new Emir Masaba said he cannot stay at Raba which was in rubbles and ashes – instead Masaba chose Lade, which is too close for comfort, to Lafiagi, as his new capital city.

With Lade as the ever-scheming Emir Masaba's new capital city, Emir Abdulkadir Manzuma of Lafiagi was virtually a captive in the hands of the all-too-power Masaba the paramount ruler of the whole of the Nupe Nation.

In fact the moment Masaba settled down at Lade as his new capital city he immediately plotted and deposed Emir Abdulkadir Manzuma that very year 1845.

Emir Aliyu Maliki's Second Term
After deposing Emir Abdulkadir Manzuma, Emir Masaba brought back Emir Aliyu Maliki from Tsonga to resume his rulership, second term, as the Emir of Lafiagi.

It bespoke of the diplomatic dexterity and mischievousness of Emir Masaba that being the one who deposed Emir Aliyu in the first place in 1834 and installed Emir Abdulkadir Manzuma in his place, he was now the same person who was able to again re-install Emir Aliyu Maliki by deposing Emir Abdulkadir Manzuma.

This story is complicated by the fact that the arch-schemer Masaba had actually used Emir Abdulkadir's brother Usman to plot the ouster of Abdulkadir from power with the promise that he will turbaned Usman as the new Emir after his brother. Albeit Masaba disappointed Usman by, instead, recalling Aliyu from Tsonga after deposing Abdulkadir.

But Emir Masaba's reign of power was suddenly cut short by his own able, but extremely powerful, war General Umaru Bahaushe.

In 1847, that is just some two years into Emir Masaba's reign, Masaba's War General Umaru Bahaushe became so powerful that, following a quarrel with Masaba over slave-raiding, he rebelled against Masaba and overthrew him from power as the Emir of KinNupe.

General Umaru Bahaushe pursued Emir Masaba from Lade through Meri to Lalagi and eventually out of KinNupe proper to Kabbaland.

Emir Abdulkadir Manzuma's Second Term
With the troublesome Masaba out of Lade, Emir Aliyu Maliki was once more deposed but this time around by Umaru Bahaushe who has declared himself as the new Etsu Nupe of the entire Nupe Nation. Umaru Bahaushe also recalled Emir

Abdulkadir Manzuma from Ilorin and reinstalled him as the new Emir of Lafiagi.

Umaru Bahaushe then sent Emir Aliyu back to his throne as the Etsu Tsonga.

And then for the next nine good years, from 1857 to 1856, Umaru Bahaushe reigned as the disputed Etsu Nupe of the whole of KinNupe.

But all the Mallams and the Etsu Nupes eventually ganged up against Umaru Bahaushe and defeated him in 1856 as he laid siege on a hapless Prince Umaru Majigi at the small walled Bini village of Bida located on the Landzun river.

Umaru Bahaushe got drowned in the River Gbako as he fled his pursuers in the dead of the night from Bida.

After the death of Umaru Bahaushe a Second Raba Convention was convened again with all the Etsu Nupes and Nupe Emirs and Mallams in attendance. At this Second Convention it was unanimously decided that all bad feelings and bitterness should be shelved among all the stakeholders of KinNupe.

At that Second Raba Convention Usman Zaki was unanimously agreed upon to be the new Emir of the Nupe

Nation. He chose Bida as his new capital city for his second term as the Emir of Nupe. Masaba was appointed as the Sarkin Fulani to Emir Usman Zaki.

Emir Abdulkadir was unanimously agreed at this Second Raba Convention to be left as the Emir of Lafiagi.

Emir Abdulkadir reigned afterwards peacefully until his death in 1868.

Emir Halilu

Upon the death of Emir Abdulkadir in 1868, Halilu was immediately turbaned as the new Emir of Lafiagi. Emir Halilu reigned for some fourteen years from that 1968 to 1882.

Emir Aliyu

Emir Halilu was succeeded by Emir Aliyu who reigned from 1882 to 1891. This Emir Aliyu was unfortunately caught up in a situation whereby he had to support the revolutionary Nupe forces who rebelled against Etsu Umaru Majigi of Bida. The rebels under Nda Legbo and Kolo Shuiabu had conquered both Tsonga and Lafiagi and held Emir Aliyu as virtually a captive.

But the rebels were eventually defeated by the Bida army supported by the Royal Niger Company forces. Emir Aliyu was therefore forced to flee Lafiagi together with the rebels to Oke Ode. The Bida forces then invaded and conquered Lafiagi.

Etsu Umaru Majigi died in 1884 while the Bida army was still occupying Lafiagi. Maliki, who was heading the Bida army at Lafiagi was, paradoxically enough, immediately installed as the new Etsu Nupe at Lafiagi.

The new Etsu Maliki was persuaded upon to let a repentant Emir Aliyu return from Oke Ode to Lafiagi.

Emir Aliyu then reigned quietly and under the shadow of Etsu Maliki until his, Etsu Aliyu's, death in 1891.

Emir Abdulrahimi
Abdulrahimi became the next Emir of Lafiagi after the death of Emir Aliyu in 1891. This Emir Abdulrahimi was the last of the biological children of Manzuma to reign as Emir of Lafiagi. Unfortunately Emir Abdulrahimi reigned for just eighteen months before he died in 1892.

Emir Ahmadu Abdulkadir
Ahmadu the son of the late Emir Abdulkadir became the next Emir of Lafiagi after the death of Emir Abdulrahimi in 1892.

During the reign of Emir Ahmadu the Nupe people of Lafiagi revolted twice against him, burnt down the town of Lafiagi and deposing Emir Ahmadu on two different occasions with the British Royal Niger Forces reinstalling him back on both occasions.

The revolt was due to the general perception in those days that the British have come over to break the power of the Emirs and Fulani dynasts over the Nupe people. In those days the British Colonial administrators, under Frederick Lugard the Anti-Nupe, deliberately balkanised the Nupe Nation and in the process excised the south-western half of the Nupe Nation which they gave to the Ilorin Province.

Emir Ahmadu died in 1915.

Emir Muhammadu Bello
Muhammadu Bello, the son of Emir Ahmadu, immediately became the next Emir of Lafiagi after the death of his father in 1915.

There was trouble as Emir Muhammadu Bello was deposed by Kpotun Shuaibu the son of the late Emir Halilu. The British authorities arrested Kpotun Shuaibu, reinstalled Emir Muhammadu Bello, and banished Kpotun Shuaibu to Katsina.

Emir Muhammadu Bello died in 1945 after reigning for a lengthy period of 30 years.

Emir Abubakar Kawu

Abubakar Kawu was turbaned as the new Emir of Lafiagi immediately after the death of Emir Muhammadu Bello in 1945. But Emir Abubakar Kawau was deposed in 1949.

Etsu Maliki

Etsu Maliki became the next Etsu Lafiagi immediately after the death of Emir Abubakar Kawu in 1949. But Etsu Maliki reigned for just a year as he died in 1951.

Etsu Abubakar

Etsu Abubakar became the new Etsu of Lafiagi in 1951 after the death of Etsu Maliki. But Etsu Abubakar abdicated in favour of Etsu Umaru Oke Ode in 1961 after a lot of allegations of misruling were levelled against the former.

Etsu Umaru Oke Ode

Etsu Umaru Oke Ode took over as Etsu Lafiagi in 1961. He reigned for fifteen years from 1961 to 1975 and his reign was considered a golden reign because it witnessed a lot of development in Lafiagi.

Etsu Umaru Oke Ode died in 1975

Etsu Sa'adu Kawu Haliru

His Royal Highness Sa'adu Kawu, the son of Mallam Haliru Lukpan, became the next Etsu of Lafiagi after the death of Etsu Umaru Oke Ode in 1975. His Royal Highness Etsu Sa'adu Kawu Haliru is still the reigning Etsu Lafiagi to date.

LAPAI EMIRATE

By the middle of the eighteenth century, that is in the 1750s, KinNupe had became the centre of the Islamic revolution in the whole of the Central Sudan. And that was almost half a millennium before the birth of Shehu Usmanu Dan Fodiyo. As I discussed in many of my books, the Islamic revolution begun in KinNupe before it spread to all other parts of ancient Nigeria.

The Etsu Nupes became the patron of the Jihadists and Islamic missionaries from all parts of Middle Africa, that is West, Central and East Africa, begun to troop into KinNupe for patronage by the Etsu Nupes.

It is on this note that Mallam Babba, an Islamic scholar from Yantumaki in today's Katsina State, left his village and came down to KinNupe. In KinNupe Mallam Babba joined the joint-Jihad efforts of Man Musa Kodogi and Mallam Dendo popularly known as Manko.

In those days the Nupe empire had shattered into two rival kingdoms headed by Etsu Jimada at Raba and Etsu Majiya II at Zugurma. These two Muslim Etsu Nupes were then using the Mallams at their respective palaces to fight battles against one another. There were lots of conspiracies, betrayals and treacheries between the various factions of Mallams and royal dynasts in those days. The story of the enmity, betrayal and eventual murder of Shehu Abdurrahman Gbaji best illustrate the diabolic nature of the situation in those days.

In the end Mallam Babba was tired of all these intrigues and dangers. He, therefore, departed from the Man Musa Kodogi-Mallam Dendo camp and went east and southwards to settle among the Dibos and Gbagyis in the general area known as Agaie today.

Mallam Babba had his own following of disciples and their families and with this he formed an Islamic commune which gradually became identified simply as Agaie community. Mallam Babba's Agaie Islamic community became the launch-pad for the vibrant proselytising of the pagan Ganagana and Gbagyi peoples in the surrounding villages. But it was not easy preaching Islam to these Ganagana and Gbagyi Nupe people who have been pagans since time immemorial.

Mallam Babba contemplated the option of organising Jihad against the pagan Ganagana and Gbagyis to convert them to Islam through wars and battles but his experiences of Jihad battles at Rabba and Zugurma under Man Musa Kodogi and Mallam Dendo discouraged him.

It was around that time that Mallam Babba heard of the death of Jaura, the Dikko or Head of the Fulanis, in a village called Maza not that far away from Agaie. Jaura was originally also from Yantumaki, the same village in Katsina from where Mallam Babba came.

Jaura was the Dikko or Head of the Fulanis at Zaria. He had wandered southwards into KinNupe in search of greener pastures for his large herd of cattle. And he was sojourning in the village of Maza among the Ganaganas and Gbagyis when he suddenly died. Umaru, who was also the Yerima to his father Jaura, became the head of the family after the death of his father at Maza.

Since Jaura was his kinsman from Yantumaki and since Maza was not far from Agaie, Mallam Babba decided to attend the funeral ceremonies of Jaura at Maza.

While at Maza, Mallam Babba and Yerima Umaru became very close friends. Sometime after the funerals, and after Mallam Babba had gone back to Agaie, Yerima Umaru decided to pay Mallam Babba a courtesy visit.

While Yerima Umaru was at Agaie Mallam Babba noticed the warlike qualities of Yerima Umaru. The two, accordingly, decided to organise Jihad battles and wars against the Ganagana and Gbagyi pagans in the surrounding areas. While Yerima Umaru was to be the war-general, Mallam Babba was to be the spiritual Islamic head of the Jihad enterprise.

Because Mallam Babba already had his own Yerima, the name of Yerima Umaru gradually changed to Shaba Maza, Shaba being the Nupe translation of the Hausa word Yerima. And since the salutation for Shaba is Daudu, Yerima Umaru became known as Daudu Maza instead of Shaba Maza.

The Jihad battles against the Ganagana and Gbagyi pagans started in earnest with General Daudu Maza conquering and converting all the neighbouring pagans into the Agaie fold of Islam.

But, and with time, General Daudu Maza was faced with some challenges. Being a very ambitious man he begun to find it more and more difficult to continue serving under Mallam Babba. And this was more so as General Daudu Maza was becoming popular as an unparalleled war-general.

In the end General Daudu Maza decided to depart from the Agaie Emirate and to go and form his own Emirate.

So, when the Battle of Fogbe took place and after the conquest of Fogbe, General Daudu Maza did not head the army back to Agaie. Instead he decided to go his own way with those among the warriors who are ready to follow him. He sent the rest of the army and the booty back to Mallam Babba at Agaie. That was in 1810.

General Daudu Maza then proceeded forward while continuing with his Jihadist battles of conquests. He conquered Kpada and Kpashimi one after the other in rapid succession. These were famous and powerful Ganagana or Dibo towns in those days.

Afterwards General Daudu Maza moved out of the Ganagana area into Gbagyiland proper and eventually settled in a Gbagyi hamlet called Pai. In the end he transformed his war-camp at Pai into a permanent settlement which became known with its full name Lapai after the nearby River Lapai in those days.

Lapai immediately grew into a famous and powerful town due to the extraordinary and remarkable personality of General Daudu Maza. The rapid growth of Lapai into a regional capital city was also aided by the continuing Jihad battles of conquests that the indefatigable General Daudu Maza continued to waged in all directions on the surrounding pagans.

Daudu Maza conquered the important Gbagyi settlements of Duma, Shaku, Gawu, Bukwo and many other smaller Gbagyi settlements in remarkable succession. And he built Paiko into a Nupe outpost town in the midst of the Gbagyi people. Minna, Bosso and many nearby Gbagyi villages were converted into more or less Nupe settlements through the influence of Paiko the Nupe town.

After an abortive attempt at conquering Abaji, however, General Daudu Maza retired back to Lapai and deputised the Jihad office to his subordinates. He was very old by then and he never personally went out on any Jihad battle thereafter.

Instead Daudu Maza concentrated his attention on the building of Lapai into a befitting capital city. He embarked on the construction of a majestic and magnificent palace in the centre of Lapai town. He completed the palace in 1825 the year he officially and ceremoniously declared himself the first Emir of his newly-founded Lapai Emirate.

General Daudu Maza the Great died in 1832.

He was officially succeeded by his very young son, Muhammadu, but was in practised succeeded by his, Daudu Maza's, brother Yunusa as the regent.

Yunusa dan Jaura reigned for six years but after his death in 1835 the people of Lapai were against Jantabo the next brother in line of succession. The people chose Hassan Baji Yadede as the next Emir of Lapai.

Jantabo became so angry he left Lapai and went on to build his own town the ruins of which are known, to this very day, as Birnin Jantabo.

But Jantabo didn't have to complete the building of his pet town for he was able to overthrow his brother Hassan Baji from power through court intrigues that were the order of the day in those days.

Jantabo dan Jaura came back to Lapai and, to the surprise of the people of Lapai, reigned as one of the greatest and a most proficient Emir that have ever ruled over Lapai. He reigned for thirty-six solid years and in that period built and established Lapai into a great and marvellous power. He was extremely warlike and expanded the territorial expanse of Lapai in all directions. Lapai became a regional Emirate power to be reckoned with.

Jantabo died in 1874.

After the death of Jantabo he was succeeded by his son Atiku. But Atiku died a year later. Atiku was succeeded by Jantabo's second son Abdullahi Bawa. However Abdullahi

Bawa was accused of not being a capable ruler. Abdullahi Bawa died three years into his reign in 1893.

Emir Abdullahi Bawa was succeeded by Emir Abdulkadir who was rejected by the people of Lapai. Abdulkadir had to abdicate in 1907. He was succeeded by Ibrahim.

Emir Ibrahim dan Jantabo was a maximum ruler. He was also opposed to the White people who were then establishing the foundations of their colonial government in Northern Nigeria. The White people hated him and cut off parts of the Lapai Emirate in order to weaken the power of Emir Ibrahim. Emir Ibrahim died in 1923.

Emir Ibrahim was succeeded by Emir Aliyu Gana. It was under his reign that the capital city of the Lapai Emirate was shifted from the original Lapai to Baddegi-Lapai (now known simply as Lapai). Emir Aliyu Gana died in 1937.

Emir Alhaji Umaru succeeded Emir Aliyu Gana. Emir Alhaji Umaru died in 1954. He was succeeded by Emir Alhaji Muhammadu Kobo who was a great grandson of Daudu Maza. Alhaji Muhammadu Kobo died in 2002 and was succeeded by the currently reigning Emir Umaru Bago Tafida.

PATIGI

KinNupe was known, in very prehistoric times, as Afa. This national name Afa was also variously pronounced, due to dialectal and geographical differences, as Apa and also as Ifa. So, KinNupe was also known in ancient times as Apa or as Ifa. The Idoma and Igala people pronounce the name as Apa to this very day while the Yoruba and Edo-Benin people still pronounce it as Ifa or Ife to this very day.

Origin of the Name 'Patigi'

The Idoma, the Igala and many other ancient Nigerian tribes said they originated from Apa. They said that they originally came from Wapan, another name of Apa, which was an almighty kingdom or empire located, once upon a time, here is Central KinNupe. The Idoma, the Igala and others migrated out of Central KinNupe a long time ago, in those days when KinNupe was known as Apa or Wapa.

Similarly the Yoruba people said that they originated from Afa, Ifa or Ife a long time ago. The Yoruba people originally migrated out of Central KinNupe in those far off days when KinNupe was knonw as Ife or Ile Ife. In Nupe, and some Yoruba, traditions Ile Ife is pronounced as Elemkpe.

We see, from all the above, that KinNupe was originally known as Apa, Afa, Ifa or Ife.

In fact KinNupe was popularly known in former times as Ifa. But Ifa was also progressively pronounced as Nyifa, Nifa, Nufa, Nufe or, as we pronounce it today, Nupe.

Yes, the modern national name Nupe is a variant of the age-old Ifa. In other words the Nupe people were also known in ancient times as the Ifa people.

In those days when the Nupe people were known as the Ifa KinNupe was known as Fati. In Old Nupe the word Eti refers to the ground, land or the earth so that Ifa-Eti or, simply, Fa-ti or Fati refers to 'Ifaland', that is, our modern Nupeland.

This Fati, for Nupeland or KinNupe, was also denominated as 'Fatigi' or, as a dialectal variant, as 'Patigi' since 'f' and 'p' are synonymous phonemes in phonology.

Some others said that the name was originally Fatiji that is Fati combined with the suffix 'ji' which in Old Nupe refers to a river. Ifati-Ji or Fati-Ji or Fatiji was therefore a common name used to refer to Nupe settlements located on river banks.

This Fatiji was also pronounced as Patiji.

It was the White Colonial scribes who came, it is said, and transcribed Patiji as Patigi or, worse still, Pategi.

Others said the name was originally Fatizhi. That is Fati, meaning Nupeland, combined with the suffix 'ezhi' which is the Nupe affix for a town or settlement in general. But Fatizhi was also pronounced as Patizhi.

This school of thought then went on to explain that it was the Colonial scribes who transcribed Patizhi as Patiji and, later on, as Patigi.

That is an etymology of our modern name, Patigi.

There were several places with the name Fati, Fatigi or Patigi in the past. The whole of KinNupe and any Nupe settlement outside KinNupe was known as Fati, Fatigi or Patigi in the past.

Our present town of Patigi was one of these ancient Patigi settlements.

Prehistoric Patigi

Today's town of Patigi was said to have been a very ancient Patigi settlement dating back to very ancient times. Its location on the very banks of the River Niger has ensured its survival right from prehistoric through historic to modern times.

Patigi has always been a River Niger port city along a long and timeworn caravan route that traversed the length of the Central Sudan from its northernmost boundary on the reaches of the Sahara cutting across the River Niger right unto the very beaches of the Atlantic on its southernmost boundaries. So, Patigi has always been a very important settlement for the very integrity of the Central Sudan since very ancient times.

Nobody knows for sure when Patigi was founded as a settlement on the banks of the River Niger. And as far as the history of KinNupe is concerned Patigi has always been there since time immemorial.

Patigi is obviously one of the oldest settlements of KinNupe and its original name may have been lost to history. Its present name as Patigi is a descriptive name as a riverine settlement as we have explained in some details at the outset of this writeup.

The names of various Nupe settlements and capital cities have changed many times throughout the eventful prehistory and history of the Nupe Nation. It is very possible then that the name of Patigi have also changed several times in the history and prehistory of the Nupe Nation.

In that context Patigi may be one of the various capital cities of ancient KinNupe mentioned, with a different name, in the many old traditions of the Nupe people.

Patigi is evidently one of the old capital cities of prehistoric KinNupe. Nupe traditions are categorical with regard to the fact that at a time in the sixteenth century Patigi was the capital city of the entire Nupe Nation. Its strategic and historic location on the juncture of the River Kaduna with the River Niger inevitably makes Patigi one of the oldest and a most capital cities of prehistoric KinNupe.

And with its pristine name as 'Fati' Patigi is obviously one of the original 'Ile Ife' settlements mentioned in the Odu Ifa panegyrics of Yoruba divination that have survived unto modern times.

Patigi and the Songhai Empire Factor
There are Nupe traditions to the effect that one of the former Etsu Nupes shifted the capital of the Nupe nation to Patigi in the sixteenth century. Some said it was Etsu Shaba II but there are indications that the particular Etsu who established Patigi as the capital of Nupe might have also been Etsu Zaula who reigned before Etsu Shaba II or Etsu Zaula II who reigned after Etsu Shaba II.

A.R. Budgen maintained that it was Etsu Zagunla who fortified Patigi into the paramount capital city of KinNupe by the end of the sixteenth century.

Whoever might have been the Etsu Nupe that built Patigi into the capital of Nupe in the latter half of the sixteenth century the fact still remains that the Nupe Nation was a vigorously expansionist superpower in those days.

It was not just Patigi that the Etsu Nupes established in Southern Nigeria in those days. It was also in those days, at the end of the sixteenth century, that the Etsu Nupes built and established the Benin Kingdom into a regional capital of the Nupe people in southern Nigeria. In those days, and right unto the second half of the nineteenth century as recorded by Captain Hugh Clapperton, the Benin Kingdom remained a Nupe kingdom through and through.

The Etsu Nupes were also involved with the relocation of the Songhai and Borgu people – both the aristocracy and commoners – who fled the sack of the Songhai Empire by the Moroccan army. The Songhai refugees were resettled by the Etsu Nupes just across the northern banks of the River Niger not far away from the location of Patigi, a capital city of Nupe in those days, on the southern banks.

It is quite clear that Patigi was the capital city of the Nupe Nation in those days that witnessed the final fall of the Songhai empire at the end of the 16th century. The Songhai Empire was already on the decline almost a century earlier but it was the final sack of the Songhai Empire by the Moroccan army in 1591 that put a definte end to the Songhai Empire.

The sack of Songhai by the Moroccan Empire in 1591 generated serious political and population crises in KinNupe. The greater KinNupe of those days shares its border, today's Borgu border in today's Benin Republic, with the Songhai Empire. And more importatntly, the founders and royal family of the Songhai dysnats originally came from Central KinNupe. So, when the Songhai Empire fall to the menace of the Moroccan army in 1591 a serious exodus of refugees from Songhai, made up of both the royalty and commoners, headed back to Central KinNupe which they said was their original homeland.

This large number of Songhai refugees thronging into Central KinNupe led to the rise and fall of different Nupe kingdoms and subtribes within and on the fringes of the Nupe Nation. It was, for instance, the days of Queen Amina of Zaria who was a Nupe woman and who was by then sitting on her throne at the Nupe town of Dunguru, now known as Zungeru, just a few kilometers away from Bida. She was the daughter of the King or Kuta, also pronounced as Guta, Kanta or Akanda, of Dunguru otherwise known as AtaGara.

But Queen Amina had to abandon Dunguru, the capital city of AtaGara, for Gbara for the fact that there was a catastrophic dispersal of the population of Central KinNupe in those days. The people of AtaGara were mostly of the ancient Yisazhi or Kisra Nupe ethnicity of the general Bini Nupe stock. The sudden arrival of the Songhai refugees to Central KinNupe resulted in the scattering of the Yisa Nupe people in different directions from their capital at Dunguru or Zungeru to other places within and outside KinNupe.

A few decades after the death of Queen Amina of Zaria the Nupe woman the AtaGara kingdom, known to the Nupe locals as the Biniya, had already crossed the River Niger and was located in the very place that came to be known to historians as Old Oyo or Oyo Ile or Katunga.

Apart from the AtaGara or Oyo kingdom the massive influx of the Songhai refugees led to the southward shifting of several Nupe kingdoms, capital cities and peoples from Central KinNupe across the River Niger to the trans-Niger half of the Nupe Nation.

Such was it that many Nupe kings, dynasts and royalties were also pushed out of Central KinNupe by the cataclysmic political and demographic changes generated as the aftereffects of the collapse of the Songhai Empire many of which citizens, particularly the eastern half of Songhai Empire, simply translocated themselves back to KinNupe their original homeland.

It was in this context that Etsu Zaula, or Etsu Shaba II, or Etsu Zaula II or even, maybe, Etsu Zagunla migrated southwards across the River Niger to establish his base at Patigi which has always been a very ancient capital city of the Nupe Nation since time immemorial.

And so was it, according to these lores, that Patigi was a capital of the Nupe Nation for a while at the end of the sixteenth century until the Etsu Nupes were said to have shifted the capital once again from Patigi to another city.

For now we don't know why the Etsu Nupes suddenly abandoned Patigi as a regional capital city of Nupe. But the traditions are quite clear that Patigi immediately became desolated and sank back into being a small town, a deserted capital, after the departure of the Etsu Nupes.

Etsu Masaba and Patigi

But then the location of Patigi as an important port-town on the banks of the River Niger eventually re-attracted the forces of Nupe history back to it again. This time it was in the middle of the nineteenth century, that is, some two and a half centuries after the Etsu Nupes shifted the capital away from Patigi at the end of the sixteenth century.

It was Etsu Masaba, that ever recurrent character in Nupe history, who, in 1835, built Lade into the new capital city of the Nupe Nation.

When Usman Zaki became the Emir of Nupe at Raba in 1833 his junior Masaba became embittered when he was not appointed as the Shaba to Emir Usman Zaki.

Etsu Masaba revolted against his elder brother's rule as the Emir of Nupe and actually raised a force against his brother at Raba. Bur Usman Zaki's powerful Raba army defeated Masaba's ragtag army at Raba and then at Pati Tuwagi.

Masaba, however, didn't relent. He went and incited the ancient Nupe dynasts, contenders to the Tsudi royal throne, against Emir Usman Zaki. These were Etsu Majiya and Etsu Idirisu. In fact Masaba joined forces with these Tsudi dynasts and their combined forces engaged Emir Usman Zaki's army at Takuma near Mokwa. But the powerful Raba army of Usman Zaki defeated, actually crushed, the combined armies of the triumvirate of Etsu Majiya, Etsu Idirisa and Masaba at that decisive Battle of Takuma in 1834.

So crushing was the defeat of the son of Etsu Idirisu and the grandson of Etsu Zubairu Majiya II were caught by the Raba army and held as prisoners of war under Emir Usman Zaki at Raba. Thus, and as we shal discuss in greater details in a later section of this work, began the Captivity Period of the Jimada dynasty under the Dendo dynasts at both Raba and Bida. This, of course, is a major chapter in the history of the foundation of the Patigi Emirate in latter times.

After being decisively crushed the Raba army of Emir Usman Zaki the triumvirate fled in different directions: Etsu Majiya fled to Zugurma, Etsu Idirisa to Edun, and Masaba fled across the River Niger to Lafiagi.

But the then Emir of Lafiagi, Emir Aliyu, refused to welcome or accommodate the rebellious Masaba at Lafiagi as doing so will simply pitch him, Emir Aliyu, against the powerful and dreadful Raba army of Emir Usman Zaki.

It was the Lafiagi Prince Abdulkadir, son to the then late Emir Manzuma of Lafiagi, who eventually took the risk of briefly and surreptitiously accommodating Masaba at Lafiagi. But even Prince Abdulkadir had to ultimately conduct Masaba out of Lafiage and took him to Patigi.

But even Patigi was too dangerous for Masaba to stay at. At Patigi Masaba will be too vulnerable to assassination by secret agents of the all too powerful Emir Usman Zaki at Raba. So, and in the end, Masaba didn't settle down at Patigi but went and settled at Lade which is just some five miles from Patigi. Lade is actually more or less a suburb of Patigi.

At Raba, however, Masaba in his characteristic persistent manner didn't forget about toppling his elder brother the powerful Emir Usman Zaki at Raba. Masaba instead became very busy at Raba plotting against his elder brother Emir Usman Zaki at Raba.

Though he was initially busy plotting against Emir Aliyu of Lafiagi who had refused to welcome or accommodate him at Lafiagi, Masaba later on, after using Sultan Halilu of Gwandu of the Eastern Half of the Sokoto Caliphate to topple Emir Aliyu of Lafiagi from power, eventually came to focus his attention on how to get his elder brother Emir Usman Zaki at Raba from power.

At that time Etsu Majiya had died and his son Etsu Tsado, at Zugurma, had became a great power to be reckoned with in KinNupe. Etsu Tsado was in possession of some of the royal regalia of Tsudi including the famous bronze Kakati royal trumpets that Tsudi fled with from AtaGara.

This Etsu Tsado was a man of remarkable and formidable personality. He was the only sort of strong-willed character who could fight Emir Usman Zaki in a courageous manner. Masaba in due time became close friends with Etsu Tsado and joined forces with him to fight Emir Usman Zaki. A series of battles between the combined forces of Masaba and Etsu Tsado against the Raba army of Emir Usman Zaki ensued.

In this series of battles the Raba army of Emir Usman Zaki was repeatedly defeated by Etsu Tsado's forces supported by Masaba. In the end Etsu Tsado and Masaba marched against Raba. Emir Usman Zaki fled Raba in the dead of the night and only escaped death by the whiskers. But Masaba together with Etsu Tsado, laid Raba to waste and reduced it to ashes when they besieged Emir Usman Zaki in the disastrous Battle of Raba. That was in 1841.

After the defeat and exile of Emir Usman Zaki the victorious Masaba declared himself the new Emir of Nupe. Masaba then used his great wealth and supreme diplomatic skills to convene the first Raba Convention whereby all the power stakeholders in KinNupe, including all the Tsudi dynasts and the Fulani emirs, were convened at a grand reconciliation meeting at Raba chaired by the Sultan Halilu of Gwandu.

At that First Raba Convention in 1841 Masaba was declared the new Emir of Nupe while Usman Zaki was exiled to Gwandu. Etsu Tsado was also declared as the rightful Etsu Nupe.

But after the Raba Convention Etsu Masaba could not stay at Raba which he himself and Etsu Tsado have completely reduced to ashes and rubbles. So, Masaba crossed the Niger and and went back to Lade which he then established into his new capital.

Incidentally Lade is just too close to Patigi – just five miles away from Patigi.

The truth of the matter, actually, is that Patigi was the original target of Etsu Masaba as his new capital. Being fully aware of the ancient history of Patigi, most of the ancient history that is lost to us today, Etsu Masaba decided to cross the River Niger and establish his capital at Patigi. In those days everybody in KinNupe had known that Patigi was one of the oldest and one of the honourable capitals of the Nupe Nation.

There are actually lost traditions to the effect that the much-sought after royal regalia of Tsudi which the ancient Tsudian dynasts have successfully hidden from the Fulani Jihadists, is hidden somewhere inside or around the vicinity of the town of Patigi. Though others are variously saying these same potent royal regalia of Tsudi are actually hidden somewhere at Mokwa, Jebba or Gbara, the the traditions asserting that they are somewhere around Patigi are more rampant. The traditions, to this very day, are that anybody who gets his hands on these hidden royal regalia of Tsudi will definitely and certainly be endowed with the spiritual and otherwise powers to be the legitimate paramount ruler of the entire Nupe Nation.

It may be the search for these hidden royal regalia of Tsudi, or any other reason unknown to us today, that may have attracted Masaba to the trans-Niger half of the Nupe Nation where he decided to establish Patigi as his capital city of the Nupe Nation.

But, and due to other reasons still unknown to us today, Etsu Masaba ended up settling down at the suburb of Patigi called Lade. This Lade is just about five miles from Patigi and was originally an unknown hamlet. Etsu Masaba initially planned to sojourn at Lade before eventually moving into Patigi proper. But he ended up not going into Patigi and instead began to build Lade into a world class capital city.

The correct name of Lade is actually Ladi and it was even known in more ancient times as Radi. But it was the White Colonial scribes who came and wrongly transcribed the Nupe name Ladi to the Latinized Lade and that is how we wrongly pronounce the name to this very day.

The emergence of Lade as the new capital of KinNupe in 1845, however, still led to the immediate rise and revival of Patigi into a major and significant city in KinNupe again.

There were actually talks in those days of the possibility of Etsu Masaba still moving into Patigi as his definitive capital city. The historical, royal and spiritual significance of Patigi as the rightful thronecity of an Etsu Nupe were just too compelling for Etsu Masaba to have remained sojourning forever at Lade.

But just two years later into his reign as the Emir of Nupe, that is in 1847, Masaba was ousted from power and chased away from Lade by his own war general called General Umaru Bahaushe.

Umaru Bahaushe was originally a war general to Emir Usman Zaki at Raba. And in fact it actually took the intervention of Sultan Halilu at the First Raba Convention to convince General Umaru Bahaushe to remain in the Raba army that was now under the command of Emir Masaba.

As a matter of fact the Raba army practically remained at Raba and refused to follow Emir Masaba to Raba. The Raba army was then receiving orders from its commander in chief Emir Masaba at Lade.

The head of the Raba army at Raba was General Andi Boshi who was also the leading war general of Emir Usman Zaki. General Andi Boshi was very loyal to Etsu Masaba but was tragically killed in a war waged by Emir Masaba against Etsu Idirisa. After the death of General Andi Boshi Emir Masaba had to replace him with General Umaru Bahaushe.

But after fighting some three or so battles for Emir Masaba, General Umaru Bahaushe rebelled against Masaba and actually turned back from a battle fight with the Raba army and marched against Emir Masaba himself at Lade.

Emir Masaba fled Lade but Umaru Bahaushe with the Raba army burnt down Lade and then pursued Emir Masaba further through Lalagi to Ilorin. Masaba eventually became asylumed at Ilorin.

The sack of Lade by General Umaru Bahaushe led to the desolation of both Lade and Patigi back into insignificant Nupe settlements again.

And so did Patigi sunk back into the quiet little port-town that it used to be for centuries on end. That is until the forces of Nupe history revisited Patigi again, this time around, in 1898.

Islamic Patriarchy Vesrus Nupe Matriarchy

In 1898 the British Colonial authorities deliberately re-established the Yisazhi branch of the ancient Tsudi (Tsoede) dynasty by officially recognising Etsu Idirisu Gana as the 23rd Etsu Nupe of the Tsudi dynasty. The White men colonialists also chose Patigi, across the River Niger from Bida, as the new capital city of the Tsudi dynasts.

This story of the restoration of the Tsudi dynasty at Patigi in 1898 started a very long time before then. We will have to go back to the very end of the eighteenth century to narrate the story in context:

In 1795, and upon the death of the erstwhile Etsu Mu'azu, the Nupe Nation got divided into two; an Eastern half ruled by Etsu Zhimada (Jimada) and a Western half ruled by Etsu Majiya.

Etsu Mu'azu had nominated his own son as his Shaba or heir apparent before his death. But this was contrary to the ancient Nupe matriarchal practice of appointing the son of a sister, that is a nephew, as the Shaba or heir apparent.

At the beginning Nupe culture, just like all other prehistoric cultures across the world, was matriarchal. In a matrichate the line of royal succession is through female geneology. When a king dies it is the nephew of the dead king, that is the son to his sister, who succeeds the dead king as the new king. That is what is applicable in a matriarchy. And that was the way a new Etsu Nupe was chose in prehistoric KinNupe.

Even Tsudi himself succeeded his maternal uncle at Nku as the new Etsu Nupe. And Tsudi himself was succeeded, not by any of his first sons Ebako and Ebagi, but by his nephew who was the son to his sister Ramatu.

Tsudi died in 1310 but close to five hundred years later in the 1780s the influence of Islam had become overwhelming in KinNupe to the extent that the patriarchal values and traditions of Islam have overshadowed the matriarchal values and traditions of Nupe culture.

It was in acting under the influence of the patriarchal values of Islam which had became fashionable in those days that Etsu Mu'azu appointed his own biological son Audu as his Shaba or heir apparent to succeed him instead of appointing Majiya, his nephew and the son to his sister, as his Shaba or heir apparent who is to succeed him after his death.

Majiya, the nephew to Etsu Mu'azu and the legitimate Shaba or heir apparent according to olden Nupe traditions felt cheated out of his birthright. So, Majiya, the nephew to Etsu Mu'azu, rebelled against his uncle. And that was how the ancient Tsudi dynasty became divided between the Mu'azu and Majiya branches of the dynasty.

Majiya eventually marshalled a huge army and ousted his uncle from power. Etsu Mu'azu fled into exile.

With Etsu Mu'azu out of the way, Majiya became the unchallenged and undisputed Etsu Nupe. Etsu Majiya was a popular Etsu well loved by all and sundry. He reigned for ten good years that were rather prosperous for the Nupe Nation.

Etsu Majiya however appointed his own son, Iliyasu, as the heir-apparent!

That Etsu Majiya will appoint his own biological son as his Shaba or heir apparent despite his being bitterly opposed to such a practice initially bespoke of the inextricable grip of Islam on the Nupe royalty in those days.

When Etsu Mu'azu finally died his son whom he appointed as his Shaba and who immediately succeeded him as the new Etsu was unfortunately a weakling. Immediately upon the death of Etsu Majiya Etsu Mu'azu came back from exile and overthrew the weak Etsu Iliyasu from power.

In the end Etsu Mu'azu was succeeded by Etsu Jimada. But Etsu Jimada also appointed his own son as his Shaba or heir apparent.

It is clear by this time that the Etsu Nupes have completely stopped practicing the olden matrilineal system of succession of the ancient Nupe culture practiced by the earlier Tsudi dynasts.

That Etsu Jimada appointed his own son as his Shaba or heir apparent made Zubairu, who is the son of the sister to Etsu Jimada, to rebel against Etsu Jimada. Zubairu was, incidentally, from the rival family of Majiya and that is why he is known to history today as Etsu Zubairu Majiya II.

Etsu Zubairu and Etsu Jimada clashed at the fateful Battle of Ragada where Etsu Jimada was killed.

Etsu Zubairu Majiya then became the paramount Etsu Nupe ruler of the Nupe Nation.

But it was at that apocalyptic juncture in Nupe history that the Fulani Mallams arrive KinNupe.

The Nupe-Fulani Mallams
It was in the days when Etsu Zubairy Majiya, othwerwise known as Etsu Majiya II, became the paramount Etsu Nupe of

the entire Nupe Nation that the Fulani Mallams gradually rose to become significant forces to be reckoned with in KinNupe.

The most famous of these Fulani Mallams was Mallam Dendo popularly referred to as Mank or 'The Great Mallam' by Nupe traditional historians.

But apart from Mallam Dendo alias Manko there were other Mallams including most famously Man Musa Kodogi, Mallam Babba of Agaie, Mallam Maliki and his brother Manzuma of Lafiagi, and so on and on.

These Mallams were originally at Etsu Jimada's palace. Etsu Jimada was the arch enemy of Etsu Zubairu Majiya II. As we have mentioned before Etsu Jimada appointed his own son as the Shaba or heir apparent to succeed him according to the patriarchal system of succession of Islam thereby denying Etsu Zubairu Majiya II, Etsu Jimada's nephew, his birthright of being appointed as the Shaba according to olden matriarchal system of succession of ancient Nupe culture.

Etsu Jimada was the one who brought Mallam Dendo to great fame and Nupe national repute after Mallam Dendo susscessfully identified the crocodile that killed and ate Etsu Jimada's grandson.

So, and for a long time Mallam Dendo was at Etsu Jimada's palace and Mallam also successfully recruited other Fulani Mallams to the Etsu Jimada palace. All these Mallams were then supporting Etsu Jimada against his arch enemy Etsu Zubairu Majiya II.

But the elderly Fulani Mallams were seriously accused of being mediocre and charlatan Islamic scholars by the younger Shehu Abdurrahman Muhammadu Sharif Tsatsa Gbaji who was the halfcaste son of the Arab Sheikh Sharif Balarabe with a Nupe woman from the Agaie general area. The quarrel between the young Nupe-Arab Shehu Abdurrahman Gbaji and the elderly Nupe-Fulani Mallams degenerated into a deadly clash that ultimately drove the Fulani Mallams away from the palace of Etsu Jimada to the palace of his arch-enemy Etsu Zubairu Majiya II.

Mallam Dendo and all the other Mallams were initially with Etsu Zubairu Majiya II as their patron at Raba. Mallam Dendo even married Etsu Zubairu Majiya's daughter Fatimatu.

But the Fulani Mallams eventually fall out with Etsu Zubairu Majiya II too. Etsu Zaubairu Majiya II actually saw Mallam Dendo snowballing followership right there at Raba after Etsu Zubairu Majiya II saw Mallam Alimi, a similar Fulani Mallam related to Mallam Dendo, who started as an innocuous Mallam at Ilorin became too powerful to the extent that he seized power from the Yorubas and established a Fulani Islamic emirate over Ilorin.

To forestall the re-enactment of Mallam Alimi's feat at Raba with Mallam Dendo, Etsu Zubairu Majiya simply chased Mallam Dendo and his Mallams out of Raba across the Niger unto the enclave of Mallam Alimi at Ilorin.

At Ilorin the Mallams rallied under the leadership of Etsu Idirisu, also known as Etsu Isa, who was the son of Etsu Jimada who was killed by Etsu Zubairu Majiya II.

Etsu Zubairu Majiya II eventually attacked the Mallams under Etsu Idirisu at Ilorin. Etsu Zubairu Majiya II was, however, defeated at the Battle of Ilorin. In fact the Mallams chased Etsu Zubairu Majiya II back across the Niger through Raba and thence unto Zugurma.

Etsu Idirisu then settled at Edun as the paramount Etsu Nupe of the whole of KinNupe. But later on Etsu Idirisu and the Mallams had a serious quarrel and Etsu Idirisu chased the Fulans out of Edu and besieged the Mallams at Raba. The Mallams, headed by Mallam Dendo, dexterously recalled Etsu Zubairu Majiya II from exile. Etsu Zubairu Majiya II then chased Etsu Idirisu from the walls of Raba through Esa to Katcha.

But Etsu Zubairu Majiya II was disappointed when he went back to meet the Dendo dynasts at Raba. After marrying his daughters to the children of Mallam Dendo, and upon the death of Mallam Dendo, Etsu Zubairu Majiya was subjected to a palace coup when the Dendo dynasts convened a Nupe national convention, with Sultan Halilu of Gwandu chairing, at Raba.

At that First Raba Convention, attended by almost all the major stakeholders of the Nupe Nation, the Fulanis told Etsu Zubairu Majiya II that they recognised only Etsu Idirisu as the rightful Etsu Nupe because according to Islamic law of succession, Etsu Idirisu is the biological son, unlike Etsu Zubairu Majiya who is the nephew, to the late Etsu Jimada.

At that First Raba Convention Etsu Idirisu was officially recognised as the Etsu Nupe of the entire Nupe Nation. He afterwards went and settled at Gbara as the capital city of the Nupe Nation. His aim was to spend the rest of his life quietly building Gbara into a befitting capital city.

That was how Gbara, for the umpteenth time, became the thronecity of the Etsu Nupe of the entire Nupe Nation again. Professor Leo Frbenius noted that Gbara has always been a recurrent capital of the Nupe Nation since time immemorial. In other words Gbara has always been a capital of the Nupe Nation.

Gbara was a renowned capital of the Nupe Nation for several centuries before the birth of Tsudi in 1230 and it continued to be the capital of the Nupe Nation for several centuries on end after the death of Tsudi in 1310.

Now in 1832, after being declared the Etsu Nupe of the entire Nupe Nation, Etsu Idirisu went back to Gbara as his capital city of the entire Nupe Nation.

But in those days the office of the Etsu Nupe was fast becoming a de jure one as that of the paramount ruler of the Nupe Nation. It was now the office of the Emir of Nupe that was fast becoming the de facto office of the paramount ruler of the Nupe Nation. And the Emir of the Nupe Nation was Emir Usman Zaki who was unanimously declared the new Emir of Nupe, for a second term, at Raba. The Emir of the Nupe Nation was at Raba and Raba had become the de facto capital city of the Nupe Nation with Gbara merely serving as the secondary, de jure, capital city of the Nupe Nation.

It was around that time, however, that Masaba rebelled against his elder brother Emir Usman Zaki who was the Emir at Raba. Masaba was able to mischievously incite both Etsu Idirisu and Etsu Tsado under his father Etsu Zubairu Majiya II, against Usman Zaki. But in the ensuing battles, particularly the one at Takuma, the sons of both Etsu Idirisu and Etsu Tsado were caught and held captive by Emir Usman Zaki at Raba.

The Jimada Dynasts Held Captive At Bida

Mu'azu Isa, the son to Etsu Idirisu was held captive at Raba by Etsu Usman Zaki. Mischievously enough the Dendo dynasts unanimously recognized Etsu Idirisu as the rightful Etsu Nupe during the first Raba Convention chaired by Sultan Halilu at Raba in 1832. They did this to spite Etsu Majiya who had helped them drove away Etsu Idirisu from his siege on the city of Raba just a couple of weeks back. The Dendo dynasts with their Gwandu collaborators explained that as Muslims they cannot recognize Etsu Majiya, who was a nephew to the late Etsu Jimada, through the matrilineal system of ancient Nupe culture. They said they can only recognize Etsu Idirisu who is the son of the late Etsu Jimada in the patrilineal system of succession of Islam.

And, interestingly enough, even though the Dendo dynasts recognized Etsu Idirisu as the rightful Etsu Nupe they didn't rectify their diplomatic relationships with him instead they continue to keep his son Mu'azu Isa as a captive at Raba.

After the death of Etsu Idirisu the Dendo dynasts rightfully recognised their captive Mu'azu Isa as the new Etsu Nupe of the entire Nupe Nation. That was in 1840.

But even though the new Etsu Mu'azu Isa requested to be allowed to go back to Gbara, his capital city, the Dendo dynasts didn't grant his request.

The Dendo dynasts kept these Jimada dynasts of the Tsudi (Tsoede) line in captivity for so many years from their days at Raba right through their own ouster from power by General Umaru Bahaushe for nine solid years through to the days they got back to power after the death of General Umaru Bahaushe in 1857 and their, the Dendo dysnats', relocation from Raba to Bida that same year.

Both Usman Zaki and Masaba, who succeeded Usman Zaki as the Emir of Nupe at Bida, continue to hold Etsu Mu'azu Isa a captive and didn't allow him to go back to Gbara.

And so was it that even though Etsu Mu'azu Isa was bearing the title of the Etsu Nupe he was still subjected to the Emirs of Nupe, or the Fulani rulers, who by then have become the de facto rulers of the Nupe Nation.

Etsu Mu'azu Isa died a captive at Bida in the hands of the Dendo dynasts in 1872. His son, Idirisu Gana, immediately succeeded him as the next Etsu Nupe. Incidentally the following year, 1873, Etsu Masaba died and Umaru Majigi became the new Emir of Nupe.

Under the reign of Umaru Majigi, Etsu Idirisu Gana tendered his requested, as did his late father Etsu Mu'azu Isa, to be allowed to go back to Gbara. This time around Umaru Majigi allowed him to go back to Gbara. Thus ended the forty years captivity of the Jimada dynasts in the hands of the Dendo dynasts from 1834 to 1874.

Etsu Idirisu Gana then went and settled down as the Etsu Nupe at Gbara as his capital city.

Arrival of the Whitemen Colonialists

Etsu Idirisu Gana was still alive, though very old, when the White men begun to establish their Colonial Government during the reigns of Etsu Maliki and Etsu Bubakar.

In fact when the Battle of Bida took place in 1897, Etsu Idirisu Gana, with his base at Gbara, actively sided with the White men against the Dendo dynasts at Bida.

In those days the Dendo dynast at Bida had become overly powerful over the whole of the Nupe Nation and have in the process inevitably made bitter and fatal enemies for themselves throughout the length and breadth of the Nupe Nation. The Bida Emirate was an imperialist and utterly expensive emirate and almost all of its colonial possessions and vassal states and people were complaining under the heavy taxation and feudalistic system of administration of the Bida Emirate.

The Kyadya riverine and canoe people were the most embittered. Their colonization by the Bida Emirate never went down well with them and they organize several rebellions and revolutions against the Bida Emirate two of the most famous of which were the Kpanti Wars and Ganigan Revolution both of which the powerful Bida army of course crushed with military ruthlessness.

Then there were also the Northern Yoruba people including the Kabba, the Igbomina, and all of the Kukuruku people who were always revoliting against the colonial sovereignty of the Bida Emirate over them.

But even the Jimada dynasts when they finally gained their freedom and got back to Gbara continued to harbor this secret vengeance against the Bida overlords. They patiently bidded their time and their opportunity came when the White men imperialists, who were the erstwhile friends of the Bida overlords and even helped them in crushing the Ganigan rebellion of the Kyadyas, eventually had a clash of interest with the Bida overlords.

The White men imperialists led by George Taubman Goldie ended up engaging the Bida overlords in their infamous Battle of Bida which was perfectly timed to take place at a time when the Bida army had crossed the River Niger into Northern Yorubaland to crush a Kabba rebellion against their Bida rulers.

The Etsu Nupe was practically defenceless and Bida was highly vulnerable to a British Colonial attack as the Bida army was stranded across the River Niger in Kabbaland.

Etsu Idirisu Gana of the Jimada dynasty at Gbara was the one who ordered the Kyadya canoemen not to transport the bulk of the Bida army across the River Niger to go and engage the British army that was bombarding the walls of Bida with a virtually unarmed Etsu Bubakar under siege.

Etsu Idirisu Gana actually played a decisive role in the fall of Bida during the Battle of Bida in 1897.

It was in recognition of his decisive assistance to their defeat of Bida that the British Colonialists decided to fully restore the ancient Tsudi (Tsoede) dynasty by officially recognising and installing Etsu Idirisu Gana as the twenty-third Etsu Nupe of the Tsudi dynasty at Patigi.

The aim of Frederick Lugard and Taubman Goldie was to balkanise the Nupe Nation and to set the Nupe people against one another. And their creation of Patigi Emirate for the ancient Tsudi dynasts of the Jimada dynasty line was just one, among many other, such divide and rule stratagems of the White colonialists.

With the creation of the Patigi Emirate for the Tsudi dynasts the White men have effectively established a second, and very legitimate Nupe dynasty because it directly traces back to Tsudi the Founder of Nupe himself, line of rulership in KinNupe that they planned will rival, and then weaken, the Fulani or Dendo dynasts at Bida.

Modern History of Royal Succession In Patigi
In any case the very old Etsu Idirisu Gana died at Patigi in 1900.

Etsu Idirisu Gana was succeeded by his son Etsu Mu'azu Isa. In 1905 the Colonial Government gave Etsu Isa a Second-Grade Staff of chieftaincy. But it was also during his tenure that the Colonial authorities shifted the headquarters of the trans-Niger Nupe Province from Patigi to Lafiagi when they, the Colonial authorities, removed Tsaragi and Tsonga from the Ilorin Division and added them to the Nupe Province. Through those addition Lafiagi became more centrally located in the Nupe Province and the Colonial authries decided that Lafiagi should be made the new headquarters.

Etsu Mu'azu Isa died in 1923 and was succeeded to the throne by Etsu Usman Tsado. Etsu Usman Tsado was actually a brother to Etsu Idirisu Gana, the father to the Etsu Mu'azu Isa.

Etsu Usman Tsado abdicated in 1931 after allegations of misrule were levelled against him by the Colonial Government.

Etsu Umaru Gana, the son of Etsu Mu'azu Isa, then succeeded Etsu Usman Tsado. Etsu Umaru Gana ruled from that 1931 to 1966, that is for some 35 solid years.

Etsu Umaru Gana died in 1966 and was succeeded by Etsu Idirisu Gana who ruled from 1966 to 1996.

Etsu Idirisu Gana died in 1996 and was succeeded by Etsu Ibrahim Chatta who rules to date.

RABA

Raba used to be the old capital of the Nupe Nation. Raba was the last capital city of the Nupe Nation from which Bida took over. The history of the Nupe Nation cannot be written without a full and consummate mention of the role played by Raba in the shaping of the annals and history of the Nupe people.

But the problem is that Raba is hardly discussed openly in historical circles concerning the Nupe people today. Things are made to look as if Raba played little or no significant role at all in the history of the Nupe Nation. The average man on the street today get's the wrong assumption that everything about Nupe history begins and ends with Bida.

The reality, however, is that the role and part played in history of Nupe by Raba might as well be greater than that of the role Bida has been playing ever since taking over from Raba as the new capital of the Nupe Nation.

It is this relegation of the historical role played by Raba – and due to many other factors – that we deem it necessary to take a full and detail look at the history of Raba itself and role it played in shaping the history of the Nupe Nation in particular and the Nupe people in general.

As far as we can garner Raba as been around as a riverine settlement on the banks of the River Niger where we still see it today for a very long time. Nobody knows for sure when Raba was first founded or even established as a settlement where we see it to this very day.

And nobody knows who was or who were the first people to found or settle Raba. All these facts are lost to history today.

All we know is that history just came and saw Raba as established already as a small village clutching onto the banks of the River Niger in the very place we see it to this very day. In those days Raba was merely one out of a countless other similar villages all on the banks of the River Niger.

Raba was, just like all the neighbouring villages in those days, merely a fishing village and most of its inhabitants were just Nupe fishermen who ply the River Niger and other smaller rivers in the vicinity for both long and short distance trade in fish, agricultural products and merchantilic products.

In those days Raba was actually known as Wabaji. In fact Wabaji was the official and traditional name of Raba until recent historical times when it acquired the nickname 'Raba'.

The nickname 'Raba' derives from the fact that the city was a port located on the banks of the River Niger almost like an

Island. In Old Nupe 'Raba' simply means 'The Water Place' or 'Waterfront' or, in a technical sense, 'A port'.

Wabaji was a port and used referred to as such by the Old Nupe word a port, namely, Raba. That was how the name of the city came to change from Wabaji to Raba in later times. Today we all call it Raba not knowing that the real and original name of the settlement was Wabaji.

But Wabaji was itself not a proper name – it was, too, a much more ancient nickname also meaning the 'Watering Place' or the 'Waterfront Settlement'.

Well, and whatever the true or original name of Wabaji or Raba might have been, history found it rising into an important waterfront or wharf settlement for local canoes and local economic activities above its neighbouring villages. Wabaji or Raba grew into a town greater than its neighbouring villages and gradually became the connected to an international trade route that connected the Northern and Southern parts of the West African region together.

The earliest of the European explorers and expeditionists to arrive KinNupe noticed the huge volume of international trade, merchandise and traffic passing through Raba from North Africa to the rest of ancient Nigeria and the Central Sudan.

But then the rise of Raba into a great city was also aided by its choice by the kings and rulers of KinNupe in those days to use it as a convenient capital city.

The point here is that even though Raba started as a commercial centre because of its position as a port strategically located on an international trade route, it was its choice as a capital city by the Nupe rulers that really transformed Raba into a mighty and powerful city in those days.

Actually it was consequent upon the division of the Nupe Empire into two rival kingdoms between the Etsu Majiya II and Etsu Jimada factions in the 1790s that led to the political rise of Raba as a regional capital of the Nupe Nation.

While Etsu Jimada had his capitals at both Zhima and Gbara, his archenemy Etsu Zubairu Majiya II had his own capitals at Zugurma and Raba. The initial capital was at Zugurma but the commercial significance of the port town of Raba made Etsu Majiya to adopt it as a secondary capital. But then Raba immediately grew into an outmatching capital where Etsu Majiya eventually came to settle.

Mallam Dendo and his other group of Mallams were initially with Etsu Jimada at the Gbara and Zhima palaces. But after their quarrel with Etsu Jimada over the role of Shehu Abdurrahman Gbaji in the Nupe Jihad enterprise, Mallam Dendo and the other Mallams changed camps to Etsu Majiya's palace at Raba. And that was how the Raba gradually began to assumed its political significance in the history of the Nupe Nation.

Mallam Dendo and his coterie of other Mallams were the guests of Etsu Zubairu Majiya at Raba. But it was the presence of the Mallams at Raba that attracted the unprecedented political and administrative fame to Raba.

The presence of the Mallams at Raba under the aegis of Etsu Zaubairu Majiya led to the fame of Raba being established as the secondary capital city to Zugurma in the Eastern Kingdom division of the Nupe Empire that fall under the sovereignty of Etsu Zubairu Majiya.

In any case the Mallams got to settle at Raba under Etsu Zubairu Majiya at a time that the power struggle between Etsu Zubairu Majiya and his archenemy Etsu Jimada was at its peak. There was eventually the Battle of Ragada in 1825. At this Battle Etsu Zubairu Majiya defeated and killed his rival Etsu Jimada.

With the defeat and death of Etsu Jimada at the Battle of Ragada Etsu Zubairu Majiya became the sole and paramount

Etsu Nupe of the entire Nupe Nation. And Etsu Zubairu Majiya consolidated his headquarters at Raba immediately after the Battle of Ragada thereby transforming Raba into the singular capital city of the entire Nupe Nation.

That was how Raba became the capital city of the Nupe Nation.

But then Etsu Zubairu Majiya reckoned, so to say, without the devil: the influence of the Mallams under him at Raba snowballed out of all proportions and immediately overshadowed his own name and influence such that the Malllams actually constituted a paralleled government to his own right there inside the city of Raba.

The problem is that people believed in the Asiri powers of the Mallams which they assume Etsu Zubairu Majiya didn't have. It was believed that it was the Asiri magical powers of the Mallams – Mallam Dendo and his cohorts – that actually secured for Etsu Zubairu Majiya his victory over his rival Etsu Jimada at the Battle of Ragada.

In any case the Mallams became more famous and more powerful than Etsu Zubairu under whom they supposedly lived at Raba. Mallam Dendo the head of the Mallams became unavoidably far more powerful and influential than the Etsu Zubairu Majiya who hosted him at Raba. Soon tension and even clashes emerged between Etsu Zubairu Majiya and Mallam Dendo at Raba.

And this was happening at a time that another Mallam, called Mallam Alimi, rose to power by overthrowing the Yoruba kings who hosted him at Ilorin. It was soon glaring to Etsu Zubairu Majiya that if he doesn't eliminate Mallam Dendo then he is going to be overthrown by Mallam Dendo at Raba just as Mallam Alimi did to his hosts at Ilorin.

In the end Etsu Zubairu Majiya chased Mallam Dendo and his other Mallams across the Niger unto the waiting hands of Mallam Alimi at Ilorin. There soon followed the great Battle of Ilorin. Also known as the Mugba Mugba Battle, it was a great battle at Ilorin which eventually turned in favour of the Mallams who ended up chasing Etsu Zubairu Majiya back across the Niger through Raba and even beyond.

Etsu Zubairu Majiya fled Raba and Mallam Dendo came back to settle down at Raba as the new most powerful man in the whole of KinNupe. These was Etsu Isa, the son of the late Etsu Jimada, as the new Etsu Nupe and his throne-city was at Edun.

Etsu Isa was the one who helped Mallam Dendo and Mallam Alimi to defeat Etsu Zubairu Majiya at Ilorin and after the defeat of Etsu Zuabairu at Ilorin Etsu Isa became the overall Etsu Nupe of the entire Nupe Nation.

But the powers, fame and renown of Mallam Dendo at Raba after the Battle of Ilorin were such that Mallam Dendo became the undisputed most powerful man in the whole of KinNupe after the Battle of Ilorin. Etsu Isa's position as the Etsu Nupe therefore simply became de jure one.

With Mallam Dendo sitting down there at Raba as his base, Raba became the most powerful city in the whole of KinNupe.

So powerful did Mallam Dendo became at Raba that Etsu Isa ruling as the Etsu Nupe in far away Edun became threatened by the paramount powers of Mallam Dendo. Etsu Isa suddenly marched on Mallam Dendo and laid siege to Raba.

But as Etsu Isa waited outside the walls of Raba for hunger to force Mallam Dendo into surrender, the highly diplomatic Mallam Dendo was able to recall the erstwhile fugitive Etsu Zubairu Majiya to come and attack Etsu Isa at the gates of Raba. Etsu Isa fled the walls of Raba and in turn became the fugitive as Etsu Zubairu Majiya chased him around and eventually out of KinNupe.

Etsu Zubairu Majiya came back had a sumptuous festival with the Dendo dynasts at Raba. The city of Raba became even more powerful and established as the undisputed capital city of the Nupe Nation.

But while the gullible Etsu Zubairu Majiya was feasting with the Dendo dynasts little did he knew that the same children of Mallam Dendo have gone to Gwandu to collect the flag of Jihad from the overall Sokoto Caliphate thereby establishing a Dendo Emirate at Raba and thereby officially and formally rendering the Etsu Nupe position that Etsu Zubairu Majiya have been laboring for totally useless.

The Dendo dynasts established the Dendo Emirate at Raba with Usman Zaki, the second son of Mallam Dendo, as the first Emir of Nupe. This Dendo Emirate was also known as the Raba Emirate since Raba was its capital city and its official seat of power.

It was around that time, in 1932, that Mallam Dendo died and was buried at Raba. The site of his grave is marked today by a mosque built beside it.

But then Usman Zaki's reign as the first Emir of the Raba Emirate was truncated by his own restless and power-mongering junior brother Masaba. This ever-scheming Masaba connived with a disgruntled Etsu Tsado to lay siege to Raba in the disastrous and catastrophic Battle of Raba which took place in 1841.

The Battle of Raba was a very vicious one indeed as both Etsu Tsado and Masaba laid siege to Raba for several days on end expecting Usman Zaki to surrender out of hunger. But when both Etsu Tsado and Masaba later on discovered that Emir Usman Zaki have escaped they angrily razed and burnt down the entire city of Raba.

So thorough and completely did Masaba and Etsu Tsado demolished and razed Raba that to this very day, more than 170 years later, Raba has never recovered or rise back out of that total destruction.

That day, the day Raba was demolished and razed completely to the ground, is the turning point in the history of Raba – for ever since then Raba has simply remained a ghost town.

After demolishing Raba and overthrowing Usman Zaki, Masaba went down to Lade where he declared himself the new Etsu Nupe and established Lade as the new capital city of KinNupe. From there at Lade, not far away from Patigi, Etsu Masaba then settled down to rule the Nupe Nation as the overall Etsu Nupe.

But Masaba's own reign as the Etsu Nupe was truncated by his own powerful war general in the person of General Umaru Bahaushe. This General Umaru Bahaushe overthrew Masaba from powerful and declared himself as the new Etsu Nupe.

For almost a decade Umaru Bahaushe reigned as the undisputed Etsu Nupe until all the forces – the Dendo dynasts and the disgruntled Etsus from the ancient Tsoede dynasties – marshelled against him. In the series of initial battles between General Umaru Bahaushe and Umaru Majigi the small Bini village of Bida on the banks of the River Landzun suddenly assumed a strategic significance as it was a walled village into which Umaru Majigi had to take refuge from the superior army of General Umaru Bahaushe.

In any case the war eventually turned against General Umaru Bahaushe as he was defeated and drowned in the River Gbako in 1856.

After the defeat and death of Umaru Bahaushe the members of the Dendo dynasty temporarily camped inside Bida as they convened a meeting on deliberations on who should be made the new Emir of Nupe. Usman Zaki, Masaba and Umaru Majigi were all there at the meeting which was mediated by Waziri Dan Adama who was there to represent the Sultan of Gwandu.

It so happened that at those deliberations at Bida the Dendo dynasts eventually agreed that Usman Zaki should be appointed as the new Emir with Masaba as the Shaba or heir apparent. Masaba agreed and Waziri Dan Adama immediately turbaned Usman Zaki as the new Emir of Nupe. In this case Usman Zaki was serving a second term as the Emir of Nupe.

After being turbaned as the new Emir of Nupe Usman Zaki made preparations to go back to Raba. His intention was to rebuilt Raba which have been reduced to ruins back in 1841. But then Usman Zaki and all the other forces at Bida had to wait for the raining season of the year 1857 to be over before they can go back to Raba. They want to go back to Raba at a time when the dry season will be in full fledge because that will be the right time to embark on the extensive architectural and town planning projects they want to undertake to rebuild Raba.

Incidentally, and while waiting at Bida for the raining season to be over, Emir Usman Zaki and the Dendo dysnats in general were approached by the indigenous Bini people of Bida who begged them to remain in Bida and to transform Bida into the new capital city of the entire Nupe Nation. The Bini indigenes of Bida remonstrated that if Emir Usman Zaki and his forces go back to Raba they, the Bida indigenes, will be left at the mercy of remants of the defeated army of the late Umaru Bahaushe who will certainly come to inflict a fatal and devastating revenge on the inhabitants of Bida.

And then there was also the argument that instead of going back to rebuild Raba why don't the Dendo dynasts simply concentrate on building Bida since Raba had been totally reduced to rubbles and ashes.

And others said that Raba was too close to Zugurma and was therefore vulnerable to a surprise attack by descendants of the Tsudi (Tsoede) dynasty who still rule at Zugurma and who hated the Nupe-Fulani Dendo dynasts. It was observed that Bida was located in a valley surrounded by expansive plains and will therefore by impossible to attack with a surprise move.

In the end Emir Usman Zaki agreed to settling down permanently at Bida with Bida as the new capital city of the Nupe Nation. It should be noted that Umaru Majigi and Waziri Dan Adama were also in full support of transforming Bida into the new capital city of Nupe.

Members of the three royal houses of the Dendo dynasty have initially set up temporary camps in Bida which was in those days just a Bini village transformed into a large military barrack or war camp. Usman Zaki, Umaru Majigi and Masaba have each set up camps at dfferent parts of Bida and when Emir Usman Zaki decided that Bida will be the new capital of Nupe each of this three royal houses of the Dendo dynasty cleared their temporary camps and began to build magnificent and world standard palaces on the sites of their ersthwhile camps. That was in 1857.

Emir Usman Zaki then ordered all the artisans and administrative officials that they have left behind at Raba to immediately relocate to Bida. The same order was given to the artisans and officials Masaba had left behind at Lade. This was Bida was immediately overwhelmed by a massive influx of artisans and government officials and general citizenry from Raba, Lade and some other cities, towns, and villages from all the nooks and corners of KinNupe.

All these contributed in no small manner to the degeneration of Raba into the small town that we still see it is today.

TSARAGI

Ibara

In the beginning there was a very ancient Nupe people known as the Ibara or Bari. As a matter of fact Professor Roger Blench documented the fact that the Nupe people were known as the Ibara in former times and right unto modern historical times.

Local Nupe historians refer to these ancient Ibara or Bari Nupe people as the Gwagba. Nupe historians, corroborated by Sir H.R. Palmer, maintained that these Gwagba were the very ones locked in a series of power struggle with the Yisa Nupe people on the eve of the advent of the Fulani Jihadists in KinNupe.

These Ibara or Bari ancient Nupe people are probably the most autochthonous of all Nupe people. They have certainly been here in Central KinNupe long before the advent or emergence of almost all other ancient Nupe tribes and subtribes.

These Ibara or Bari Nupe people were also variously known as the Gbari, Gbwara, Gwara, Kwara, Koro, and so on and on. Sultan Bello referred to them as the Gawara. They derived their national name from the name of the River Niger, Kwara or Koro, upon which their entire sociology is centred.

Gbidigi

In latter times they were to be referred to by other Nupe subtribes as the 'Ibara edigi' which is a Middle Nupe term meaning 'The Ibara language'. This phrase 'Ibara edigi' was later on, and progressively, contracted into 'Ibaraedigi', 'Baraedigi', and, finally, into 'Baedigi' or 'Badigi'.

The ancient Ibara Nupe people thus became known as the Badigi people. And their Ibara language was then referred to Gbidigi.

It was this ancient Gbidigi Nupe language that the colonial historians transcribed as 'Gbedegi' which Professor S.F. Nadel was to come later on and said was one of the most ancient of the Nupe subtribes.

In any case, and as we were initially discussing, these Ibara, Bari, Baedigi or Gbidigi Nupe people were one of the most ancient and a most aboriginal people of KinNupe.

At a very remote time in the past, and on the authority of Professor J.E.G. Sutton and Sir C.R. Niven, these Ibara or Bari Nupe people used to be spread over the whole of not only KinNupe but almost all other parts of ancient Nigeria. They were known as the Bori people in ancient Northern Nigeria, as the Ibo in ancient Southern Nigeria, as the Kalabari (Calabar) on the Niger Delta, and so on and on.

Sultan Bello referred to these Ibara, Bari or Gwara ancient Nupe people as the Gawara people and mentioned that they actually dominated almost the whole of ancient Nigeria. Leo Africanus said the Ibara or Gara Nupe people actually dominated the whole of Northern Nigeria as recent as the 16th century.

Anyway, the entire KinNupe used to be wholly populated by these Ibara or Gbidigi Nupe people in very ancient times.

But at a latter time, and with the rise of Tsudi's (Tsoede's) Nupeko Kororofa empire, the Gbidigi people were gradually displaced and dislodged from various parts of KinNupe. And even the Gbidigi language eventually ceased to be the national language of the entire Nupe Nation.

The ancient Gbidigi people were gradually pushed out of Central KinNupe until at a time they became a minority in North and Central KinNupe and only remained a majority in Southern KinNupe.

In those days KinNupe was far larger than the KinNupe of today. In those days Southern KinNupe actually included the modern Nigerian states of Kwara State, Ekiti State, Ondo State, Edo State and Kogi State. In other words today's Northern Yorubaland was yesterday's Southern KinNupe.

And in those days the Lingua Franca spoken over the whole of Yorubaland, especially the Northern Yorubaland, was the Nupe language of Ibara, Bari or Gbidigi.

As a matter of fact the people of Oyo in those days were variously known as the Gbidigi, Bari or Biniya Nupe people. This was simply because the Oyo kingdom in those days was a Nupe kingdom through and through.

In fact the very name Yoruba is a Latinization of Yariba which is a compound of Ya and Riba. But Riba is simply a mirror-image of Bari which was, of course and as we have said over and over again in this present work, the national name of the Nupe people in very ancient times.

So, the Yoruba people were originally a Ya-Riba, Ya-Bari or Bari or Ibara Nupe people.

As a matter of fact Old Oyo was actually located right here in KinNupe. But Old Oyo was the most powerful kingdom in the whole of the Yorubaland of those days – yet Old Oyo was a Nupe kingdom.

For a very long time, and throughout the reign of Old Oyo kingdom, the Nupe people ruled over practically the whole of Yorubaland in the form of the sovereignty of Old Oyo and otherwise. And everything about Yorubaland was influenced and shaped by the Old Oyo Nupe kingdom.

That was why when the Old Oyo kingdom was sacked in the 1530s the catastrophic consequence of this was disastrous for the whole of the Yorubaland.

By the beginning of the 16th century the Nupe kingdom of Apa has grown into an empire and have became the singular superpower in Central KinNupe. From Central KinNupe this Apa empire set out to reconquer all other colonial possessions of Nupe from all parts of the Central Sudan. One of these colonial possessions was, of course, the Old Oyo kingdom of Katunga or KataGara which was a remnant of the AtaGara Nupe empire that the Apa empire have come to replace in Central KinNupe.

The official or state religion of the Apa empire is the Nupe religion of Afa or Ifa otherwise known as Eba or Ebasan in modern day KinNupe. The lords of this new Apa empire imposed their religion of Ifa on the Old Oyo kingdom. But the Old Oyo people, who were an AtaGara or Bari or Gbidigi Nupe people, revolted against the Ifa religion of the Apa Nupe people.

The result was the sack and destruction of the Old Oyo kingdom by the Apa Nupe overlords. The then king or Alafin of Oyo was also deposed and banished to today's Borguland which was, in those days, the Western KinNupe of the Greater KinNupe.

The subtle point that needs to be elaborated here is the fact that the sack of Old Oyo did not only affect the Old Oyo kingdom. The sack of Old Oyo affected the whole of the Northern Yorubaland or Southern KinNupe area in general.

For instance, was not only the royal family of the Old Oyo kingdom that were forcibly repatriated back to the Western KinNupe of those days. As a matter of fact an overwhelming population of the Gbidigi Nupe people of Northern Yorubaland were repatriated en masse back to Western KinNupe. It was ever since then, to this very day, that the Western half of KinNupe – the trans Kaduna axis starting from roughly the 5'30 longitude – became the enduring bastion of the Gbidigi Nupe people as it remains to this very day.

It was from those days that places like the Jebba, Mokwa, Bokani, Pizhi, Zugurma general areas became overwhelmed by Gbidigi population.

Mokwa in particular began its rise to historical prominence in those days. Of course Mokwa has been around for a long time before those mid-15th century days. But the massive influx of the Gbidigi people from the south unto the Mokwa general area transformed Mokwa into a renowned town. The strategic location of Mokwa on the trans-Saharan trade route that continued right down to the Atlantic Ocean also contributed a lot to the prominence of Mokwa in those days.

The point is that in those days Mokwa was a great city. Even before Shehu Abdurrahman Gbaji, otherwise known as Abdurrahman Tsatsa, tried to convert Mokwa into the seat of the Nupe Caliphate, Mokwa was a big and cosmopolitan Nupe settlement. A lot of people were migrating into and out of Mokwa.

It is evident that it is one of those in and out migration of ancient Nupe peoples that led to the migration of the Mulia Gbidigi people into and out of Mokwa on their way to the other bank of the River Niger where they finally settled and found the great city of Gudu.

It was called Gudu because it was located on the River Niger. Gudu was another ancient Nupe name for the River Niger or any river in general. Gudu is actually a shortened formed of Guduru which is an Old Nupe word meaning 'river'.

And these ancient Nupe people, who built and settled in Gudu, became popularly known as the Kpwatwa or Kpoto people. Kpwatwa or Kpoto simply referred to the River Niger on which they established the port city of Gudu. Actually Kpoto, Kpwatwa, Kwata or Kpata is used in Modern Nupe to refer to a waterfront, waterside or a port.

In any case Kpoto refers to their riverine lifestyle with which they became famous when they built their great city of Gudu on the banks of the River Niger.

The man who led these Kpoto people from Mulia through Mokwa to Gudu was known as Ndace Dogun.

Gudu grew into a great and mighty city under the leadership of a Kpoto king called Lazhi.

The rapid growth of Gudu obviously became a threat to other Nupe regional powers. It was said that the almighty Etsu Nupe of those days ended up attacking Gudu. The Etsu Nupe actually sacked the great city of Gudu and ever since then the city has remained in ruins to this very day.

The modern village of Gudu or Ogudu only came about after the Royal Niger Company encamped beside the ruins of ancient Gudu.

The Kpoto people of Gudu fled further south and, in their scattered flight, ended up founding three daughter settlements, namely, Ndakogonshi, Kpotofu Tayechin and Dumagi.

Ndakogonshi and Kpotofu Tayechin are now in ruins.

Ndakogonshi was located close to the present town of Tsonga and in fact its ruins can still be seen on the Patigi Gonshi hill close to Tsonga.

Kpotofu Tayechin was located not far away from the present village of Zambufu. The ruins of Kpotofu Tayechin are also to be seen to this very day.

Dumagi is still a flouring town to this day.

Of the three original towns founded by the Kpoto people who fled Gudu, Kpotofu Tayechin was the biggest for the simple reason that both the children of the ruling houses of the Ndace Dogun and Lazhi settled at Kpotofu Tayechin.

Soon Kpotofu grew into a big settlement – in fact it became the new Gudu.

So big and important did Kpotofu became that the Etsu Nupe was soon forced to recognise it as a great power to be reckoned with. The Etsu Nupe appeased the reigning Lazhi of Kpotofu by ceding to him the whole of the Gudu general area which included the places where the present towns of Tsonga, Tsaragi (or Share) and Ogudu are located. The Zambufu district was not part of it though.

The Etsu Nupe turbanned the Lazhi as the Ndakpoto. The Ndakpoto ruled over the whole of the Gudu Province including all the towns we have mentioned above. And the Ndakpoto in turn paid annual tribute to the Etsu Nupe.

By the beginning of the 19th century Kpotofu was already a great city and a regional capital of the Nupe people.

And it was around that time, circa 1800, during the reign of Ndakpoto Ahmadu Saba, that a group of Igbomina hunters fleeing the Ibadan wars, came and sought asylum under the Ndakpoto in Kpotofu.

Ndakpoto Ahmadu Saba accommodated the Igbomina refugees in a Kpotofu suburb called Sakama. The Ndakpoto also gave the chief hunter of the Igbomina refugees the title of 'Olukpako'.

'Olukpako' is derived from 'Olu Kpakonyakpa' and is a Nupe royal title given to the Igbomina or Yorubanized Nupe settlers. Even the very etymology of this royal title proves the fact that the Igbomina were a subject people to the Nupe people of today's Tsaragi.

The refugee Igbominas became a people completely subject to the Ndakpoto Ahmadu Saba who, out of goodwill, have accommodated them in his own capital city of Kpotofu.

But around that time the Rebel Mallams of Raba headed by Mallam Dendo and Man Musa Kodogi were, under the aegis of Etsu Idrisa who was the son to the slain Etsu Jimada, gathering a formidable army at Ilorin with Mallam Alimi for an all out war against Etsu Majiya.

There was widespread rumour of war in those days that the Battle of Ilorin between Etsu Majiya and the Etsu Idrisa who is with the Rebel Fulani Mallams will drastically affect Kpotofu.

The story was that Ndakpoto Ahmadu Saba and his Kpotofu warriors were also implicated in the death of Etsu Jimada (Etsu Zhimada) at the disastrous battle of Ragada just a couple of kilometres from Patigi. Now Etsu Idrisa and the Fulani Mallams are not only seeking for revenge on Etsu

Majiya but also on all his allies which included Ndakpoto Ahmadu Saba and the people of Kpotofu.

With this turn of events Ndakpoto Ahmadu Saba fled the city of Kpotofu and went and encamped at the location of the present town of Tsaragi. In those days Tsaragi was just an hamlet but it was located near a hill to which Ndakpoto Ahmadu Saba and his people could easily seek refuge in case of an overwhelming attack.

Ndakpoto Ahmadu Saba also brought his Igbomina subjects with him from their Sakama ward in Kpotofu. He camp them in another hamlet called Share which was located just beside the Tsaragi hills where Ndakpoto Ahmadu Saba had fled.

It turned out that Etsu Idrisa and his Fulani Mallams didn't attack Kpotofu during the Battle of Ilorin. But then Ndakpoto Ahmadu Saba didn't go back to Kpotofu, instead he immediately built and established Tsaragi into a big and great city.

So, and in essence, we can see that the journey of these Kpoto Nupe people which had begun from their ancestral town of Mulia have passed through the stages of Mokwa, Gudu, Kpotofu and, eventually, have permanently settled at

Tsaragi which has remained their base and headquarters to this very day.

But by this time the reins of Nupe sovereignty have passed from the Tsoede dynasts at Gbara to the Dendo Fulani dynasts at Raba.

The Fulani Jihadists and the Dendo dynasts in particular continue to feel uneasy about the Ndakpoto and his Tsaragi kingdom even after the victory of the Fulani Mallams at the Battle of Ilorin.

It is in this regard that, and to the chagrin of the people of Tsaragi, Usman Zaki when he became the first Emir of Nupe recognised the Olukpako of the Igbomina refugees as a chieftaincy title of the Etsu Nupe. This, in a sense, gave the Olukpako some autonomy from the sovereignty of the Ndakpoto.

But more damaging to the Ndakpoto's or Etsu Tsaragi's authority was the calculated manner in which the Fulani Jihadists cut and shared the Gudu Province of the Ndakpoto into independent fiefdoms they, the Fulani authorities, set up after their establishment as the paramount rulers of the Nupe Nation.

In 1834, and with the machinations of Etsu Masaba the Great who was then on exile at Ilorin, the Emir Halilu of Gwandu of the Sokoto Caliphate drastically reduced the sovereign powers of the Ndakpoto or Etsu Tsaragi by deliberately excising great parts of his erstwhile Gudu Province and giving them away as gifts to newly empowered emirs, chiefs and ajeles.

The Tsonga part of the Gudu Province of the Ndakpoto or Etsu Tsaragi was given away to the then deposed Emir Aliyu of Lafiagi. Emir Aliyu subsequently set up his Tsonga Emirate.

The remaining parts of the erstwhile Gudu Province of the Etsu Tsaragi the Emir Usman Zaki shared as fiefdoms among his loyalist Ajeles in Share and Dumagi. Usman Zaki also appointed an Ajele at Zambufu.

But all these did not calm Etsu Masaba's spite for the Ndakpoto and the people of Tsaragi. When Masaba became the Etsu Nupe with Lade as his capital city he came and drove almost all the Nupes out of Tsaragi and thereby leaving only the Igbominas as the overwhelming inhabitants of the town.

In 1850 the Ndakpoto or Etsu Tsaragi and half of his Nupe subjects were pursued by Masaba from Tsaragi through Zambufu and Kusoko to Dumagi.

The other half Nupe population of Tsaragi fled to the Jebba area.

After three years in exile Etsu Masaba eventually allowed the Nupe people of Tsaragi to return back to Tsaragi.

But when the Nupes returned to Tsaragi they discovered, to their shock, that the Fulani dynasts at Bida have appointed the Olukpako leader of the Igbomina refugees as the paramount chief of Tsaragi. The Ndakpoto merely became a title below the Olukpako.

It was a period of ignominy for the Nupe people of Tsaragi until the White men came and conquered the Fulani rulers at Bida.

The White men reviewed the history of Tsaragi and Share and decided to restore the sovereign powers of the Ndakpoto or Etsu Tsaragi – powers which the Fulani rulers have systematically taken away from the Ndakpoto or Etsu Tsaragi dynasts.

This opportunity came in 1905 when the Igbominas of Tsaragi quarrelled among themselves and eventually deposed their Olukpako who was subsequently exiled to Ilorin. With the Olukpako deposed as the paramount chief of Share or Tsaragi, the White men colonial administrators restored the

Ndakpoto or Etsu Tsaragi as the paramount ruler of both Tsaragi and Share.

The Ndakpoto at that time was called Gonshi, he was the son of Ahmadu Saba and was the successor to Ndakpoto Abubakar who died in 1902.

Ndakpoto Gonshi was accorded a 3rd Grade Staff of Office by the White men colonialists in 1909. From 1910 to 1917 the colonial administrators also reclaimed for the Ndakpotos some of the Gudu districts the Fulani rulers seized from them. The colonial administration also added the Zambufu district to the Tsaragi Emirate.

The White men colonial administrators also categorically maintain that the Olukpako must serve under the Ndakpoto or Etsu Tsaragi. That the Olukpako is subject to the Ndakpoto was clearly delineated and stipulated by the colonial administration when it was discovered, in 1917, that the Emir of Ilorin had secretly told the Olukpako not to defer to the Ndakpoto or Etsu Tsaragi.

But the same colonial administrators excised Share and Zambufu from the Tsaragi area in 1945.

Postscript: Tsaragi is Nupe not Yoruba

Tsaragi is the only town in Nigeria that is completely bilingual - Nupe and Yoruba - both in language and in population. Tsaragi was, however, founded by the Nupe people as they fled the endless wars and scheming of Etsu Masaba in the middle of the 19th century.

When Ndakpwatwa Ahmadu Saba, the famous Etsu Tsaragi in the late 1860s, moved his people from their original settlement he also brought along with him his Yoruba, actually Igbomina, guests whom he have granted asylum to earlier on at his original settlement. That was how the Yoruba people came to be part of Tsaragi - they were originally the refugee subjects of the Ndakpwatwa.

The Igbominas have come to KinNupe originally as refugees fleeing the Ibadan wars and the terminal crises of Abeokuta. They arrived as refugees at Kpotofu the initial city of the people of today's Tsaragi. The Etsu Tsaragi Ndakpwatwa Ahmadu Saba granted the Igbomina or Yoruba refugees asylum in a part of Kpotofu called Sakama.

It was while fleeing the impending attack of Etsu Masaba, during the wars of Masaba with his elder brother Usman Zaki, that the then Etsu Tsaragi Ndakpwatwa Ahmadu Saba left Kpotofu with all his Nupe citizens and his Igbomina subjects to the Tsaragi area where he eventually founded the present town of Tsaragi. Etsu Tsaragi Ndakpwatwa Ahmadu Saba then settled his Igbomina or Yoruba subjects, whom he have brought along with him, in a part of his new town of Tsaragi.

Tsaragi was named after a then nearby river called Tsara which the Yoruba people pronounced as Shara or Share. And that was how the Yoruba people corrupted the original Nupe name Tsaragi or Tsara into Shara or Share as they call it to this day.

Even after Etsu Tsaragi Ndakpwatwa Ahmadu Saba as founded Tsaragi as his new settlement, the Igbominas remained his subjects and slaves.

But in those days the Nupe-Fulani rulers at Bida didn't like the Ndakpwatwa rulers of Tsaragi and so they used the infamous 'divide and rule' strategy to undermine the power and authority of the Etsu Tsaragi by empowering the Igbomina Yoruba slaves against their Nupe masters at Tsaragi.
It was Etsu Masaba, in conjunction with the Fulani overlords back in Gwandu, who schemed to upgrade the Igbominas or Yoruba royal and chieftaincy titles, including the Olukpako, with which the Yorubas later on revolted against their Nupe masters in Tsaragi.

Now the Igbominas, referring to themselves as the Yorubas of Share, are ignominiously and shamelessly claiming that they are the founders or owners of Share and Tsaragi. They have deliberately turned a blind eye on the historical fact that they were originally refugees sheltered by a magnanimous Etsu Tsaragi in the 19th century.

We should note the fact that the very royal title, 'Olukpako', with which the Head of the Igbomina or Yoruba people of Share is identified to this very day, is not a Yoruba or Igbomina word but is a Nupe word. Olukpako is a shortened form of 'Olu-Kpakoro' which is itself a shortened form of 'Olu Kpakoronyaka' or 'Olu Kpakonyakpa'. Of course, and to this very day, 'Kpakonyakpa' is a salutation addressed to anybody given a titled by the Etsu Nupe. The head of the Igbominas was titled or turbaned by the Etsu Tsaragi in the 19th century.

Even the Colonial authorities, who eventually learnt the true historical origin of the Igbominas or Yorubas of Share and Tsaragi, officially subjected the Share Igbominas or Yorubas under the rulership of the office of the Etsu Tsaragi.

By the time the White men arrived and established Nigeria the Igbomina have been virtually removed from the authority of the Etsu Tsaragi through the scheming of the Nupe-Fulai rulers of Bida. But the White men, interestingly enough, re-established the authority of the Etsu Tsaragi over the Olukpako of the Igominas and made the Igbomina Yorubas of Share completely subjected to the rulership and authority of the Nupe people of Tsaragi.

It was only after Independence that the Yoruba hegemonists went back to removing the Igbomina and Yorubas of Share from the authority of the Nupe people and Etsu Tsaragi.

www.ingramcontent.com/pod-product-compliance
Lightning Source LLC
Chambersburg PA
CBHW061347250726
48657CB00004B/1371